CORPORATE SUCCESS

FOR THE MEDIOCRE

A GUIDE

And an Explainer for the Rest of Us

Arturo Bello

CosmicJustice.net Press

Published by CosmicJustice.net Press

ISBN: 0983762805
ISBN-13: 9780983762805
Library of Congress Control Number: 2011912385

CosmicJustice.net Publishing, Gibsonia, PA

About the Author

Arturo Bello has spent more than a dozen years as a manager working with large, globally focused corporations for the best-known and most selective companies in the world. As an employee or a consultant, he has known more than twenty corporate organisations with more than just passing familiarity. Being a keen observer of human interaction, with just enough knowledge about the principles of organisational behaviour from his MBA to be dangerous, topped off by a passion for social justice and good governance, he set out to document his observations in a useful handbook, in the spirit of Machiavelli's *The Prince*.

Bello's industry experience spans strategy consulting, media, telecoms, Internet, and software. He has lived and worked in the United States and in several European countries. Always a student of human nature, he seeks to make sense of the world and the forces that shape it and to learn and internalise all inputs. This is his first effort to pass on his knowledge and, perhaps, to reshape the world, in turn.

Bello enjoys travelling around Italy, gossiping with work colleagues around the water cooler, and reading fan e-mails at *Arturo.bello.no1@gmail.com*. In addition to his corporate work, he is the founder of an Internet start-up dedicated to the promotion of truth in the political arena. More information is available (including ways to purchase this book in digital or print formats) at *www.arturobello.com*. He is now working on notes for his next book, **Breaking In Your New Boss—A Guide (*How to Turn Corporate Volatility to Your Advantage*)**, which will be announced on his Web site upon publication.

Table of Contents

Introduction

The world is run by C students, it has been said, and one George W. Bush was a vivid and, by now, legendary manifestation of this principle. A man of mediocre talents, few accomplishments, and unremarkable experience rose to be President of the United States—what some would call the most powerful man in the world. His success will serve as inspiration to people of mediocre skills and abilities for decades to come. If he can do it, if he can succeed, if he can attain honours and glories, power, and, most importantly, wealth, *SO CAN YOU*.

If you have picked up this book, then it is likely that at some point you have had thoughts that perhaps you, too, are mediocre. Firstly then, you are owed a definition of this term.

But even before that, let us define what the mediocre are *not*:

- They are not lazy
- They are not stupid
- They are not incapable

If they were any of these things, they would not be mediocre. They would be, by definition, "bad". The population of the world is distributed along a normal distribution of intelligence, capabilities, and industriousness. The strong end of this spectrum contains people who are "excellent", with the "bad" at the other end (not "bad" as in evil or malicious, rather bad in the sense of "not good"). The "mediocre" occupy the middle. This is perfectly normal and, indeed, dictated by statistics themselves: the mediocre are *in the middle*, by definition of the word. The question is: being mediocre, can you still go above and beyond average success in the corporate world? A world that, at least in Western culture, prides itself on meritocracy, excellence, and the bottom line. The answer is yes, yes you can! This book lays out how.

Having established that the "mediocre" and the "bad" are not the same, here is how the "mediocre" differ from the "excellent":

- **They do not strive for excellence**—where excellence denotes a superior product, performance, or result. The mediocre have no desire or intention to achieve it, even though they might if they tried. This is more than simply a (conscious) calculation of return on investment (ROI); this is a spiritual and emotional lack of drive to be great.
- **They have no shame or pride**—which is similar to saying they do not care what other people think of them. While they are fully conscious that perception may impact relationships, and, moreover, they are somewhat aware of the opinions others have, they are willing to do or to say anything that gets them to their personal goals, regardless of the impact on their reputations.
- **They are self-centred**—all their actions revolve around improving their own lots. Only if there is an obvious benefit to themselves in contributing to a collective will they do so. Otherwise, on issues of society, shareholder value, social impact, long-term investment, and so

forth, they have no interest nor are willing to sacrifice anything of their own.

Combining the two bulleted lists above should make the dominant characteristics of the mediocre clear. (In pop culture, the main boss from the popular TV show *The Office* can be recognised as a pitch-perfect example of the above. The show could actually serve as a perfect anecdotally illustrative, and comedic, companion to this expository book.) As to *why* the mediocre are this way, let the anthropologists and psychiatrists explain. It might very well be an optimal survival strategy in both the ancestral and modern environments. But it is important to note that the mediocre are rarely introspective enough to choose such a path consciously, as a result of careful evaluation of costs and benefits.

In any case, this book deals only with manifestations of success of the mediocre in the corporate world. It explains the mechanisms, logic, rules, and tricks that can be employed to this end. Unlike the lazy, stupid, and incapable, the mediocre are quite interested in success and are willing to work hard to obtain it. Success brings all sorts of comforts, pleasures, and social recognition. The mediocre are adept and often very driven to leverage their intelligence and capabilities to pursue professional accomplishment in the corporate world. If this describes you and your interests, go straight to Chapter 1!

If you are still reading this far, you are probably not mediocre. Rather, you are likely to be from the "excellent" end of the spectrum. This book is also an explainer for you, as the cover says. You perhaps have observed corporations at which you have worked and have wondered how the mediocre can achieve such a disproportionate level of success. To you, it seems counterintuitive and, upon profound observation, even illogical that corporations and their cultures can promote people who have no interest in excellence, despite the fact that many of these companies depend on excellence to remain competitive and profitable in the marketplace. Counterintuitive that companies can promote people who regularly alienate and de-motivate their colleagues, despite the fact that many of these companies position and pride themselves on maintaining progressive emotional work environments and speak often about the importance of their human capital. Counterintuitive that companies promote people who regularly make obviously wrong or damaging decisions for the company, accept no responsibility, and completely ignore the consequences. And yet . . . you know that it happens *all the time*. Which is why you, too, are reading this book.

For you, then, this book can help understand some of the rules and logic of corporations that make such results possible. You have most likely spent your life looking at things from a particular framework—the framework of excellence—and are thus not aware of the alternate frameworks that live in corporations. If you are still early in your career, perhaps you were a straight-A student, where the logic for the first half of your life was quite simple: go to class, pay attention, do your homework, study for your tests, get a good grade, graduate with a high GPA, get honours and accolades, and even get a job offer at a good company. Do good work → get recognised → get rewarded. Simple?

Perhaps you also studied economics and came to believe in the efficient allocation of resources, the constructive creation of value, and the concept of fair pricing. Or you studied history, replete with examples of people of excellence and genius—inventors, politicians, writers who get statues and everlasting respect. And you concluded that the modern engine of global advancement—the Western corporate world—must also operate by these principles, lest millennia of progress and learning be wasted and void. If you have not already, you will find that the corporate world is nothing like you thought it would be. The best people are *rarely* in charge, the mediocre *regularly* get rewarded disproportionately to their contributions, and corporate organisations *invariably* decay their levels of excellence over time. Clear your preconceptions, and read on to Chapter 1!

If you are still reading here, then you are diligent enough to be rewarded with this book's definitions of "Corporate" and "Success". Regarding "Corporate": this book examines a specific segment of society—namely, Western (European, North American) commercial entities of large or medium size. Typically, companies with more than two hundred employees are included in this category (one good rule of thumb is that the company is large enough that the CEO no longer knows everyone's name). What makes this segment particularly interesting is that a very large proportion of the Western workforce is employed by such companies and that they drive a very large proportion of economic activity in the West. Therefore, they are a fundamental actor in culture, society, economics, and progress. In this book, "Corporate" is not the same as incorporated, nor does it even mean for-profit; however it does exclude clubs and associations. Essentially, consider it to mean *any organisation with more than two hundred people who are paid to be there for the majority of their working hours.*

The definition of "Success" is simpler: this is comprised of promotions, raises, recognition, awards, and increased rights (not necessarily responsibilities). (Even all this can be essentially abridged to, simply, promotions. Promotions typically entail long-term increased compensation, rights, recognition, and so forth. Corporations are rarely able to bestow any of the other elements of Success piecemeal without soon equalising them with a corresponding promotion.) In this book, consider success to *mean promotions and permanent salary increases.*

Most people who work want Success, and many of you work in the Corporate world. Among the millions and millions of people who are in this cross-section, many are mediocre. The author hopes this book can be helpful to them and explanatory to the rest of us.

CHAPTER 1
Results Don't Matter

This chapter is first in the book for a reason. If you remember nothing else from this book, remember this one thing—results don't matter. Do not worry about achieving your metric targets. Do not worry about delivering your quarterly commitments. Do not worry about your bottom line. If you are at any organisational level at which your manager's manager knows your name, you are already at the level where results simply don't matter.

If results mattered, would the Wall Street and City bankers responsible for the collapses and defaults of their companies have walked away with hundreds of millions of dollars, in some cases even getting new jobs in the same industry? Would Richard Fuld, former chairman and CEO of bankrupt Lehman Brothers, have made $490 million from selling Lehman stock in the years before the company filed for Chapter 11 bankruptcy?[1] Would Howard Hubler, who appears

---

1   Barry Ritholtz, "Putting an end to Wall Street's 'I'll be gone, you'll be gone' bonuses," *The Washington Post*, http://www.washingtonpost.com/wp-dyn/content/article/2011/03/12/AR2011031204299.html   (2011). Further fascinating statistics are given in this article, notably: "Countrywide Fi-

to have single-handedly (if you discount the ignorance of his bosses) lost Morgan Stanley *$9 billion*, "more than any single trader has ever lost in the history of Wall Street", have been rewarded with a penny, let alone the tens of millions of dollars in pay he took away?[2] In the just slightly smaller magnitude world of London, would "Sir" Fred Goodwin have been paid about $10 million in 2007 and then permitted to keep tens of millions in pension payouts, despite producing the largest annual corporate loss in UK history (£24bn in 2008) and having knocked approximately 85 percent off the stock price during his tenure as CEO of Royal Bank of Scotland?[3] Would Lord John Browne have been invited to be the most senior director of the business management team in the UK government at exactly the same time that British Petroleum, the company he chaired for a decade, was facing market collapse (more than $100 billion in market valuation wiped out) due to his legacy of dismantling safety enforcement and lax regulatory compliance, culminating in the Gulf of Mexico oil spill of 2010?[4] These examples are used because they come from well-documented and highly publicised recent news stories. But they illustrate that even at the highest levels of the most ostensibly bottom-line-oriented businesses in the world, **results don't matter**.

---

nancial (now owned by Bank of America) founder and CEO Angelo Mozilo cashed in $122 million in stock options in 2007; his total take is estimated at more than $400 million dollars. Stanley O'Neal, who steered Merrill Lynch into financial collapse before it was taken over in a shotgun wedding with Bank of America in 2008, was given a package of $160 million when he retired. Bear Stearns former chairman Jimmy Cayne, rescued by a $29 billion Fed shotgun wedding to JPMorgan Chase, received $60 million when he was replaced."

2   Max Abelson, "Howie Hubler of New Jersey: The Return of a Subprime Villain," *The New York Observer*, http://www.observer.com/2010/wall-street/howie-hubler-new-jersey-return-subprime-villain (2010).

3   "Fred Goodwin," *Wikipedia*, http://en.wikipedia.org/wiki/Fred_Goodwin (2011).

4   Tom Bower, "Return of Lord Oil Slick: Why has Cameron handed this Labour luvvie such a key job?", *The Daily Mail*, http://www.dailymail.co.uk/debate/article-1291663/Return-Lord-Oil-Slick-Why-Cameron-handed-Lord-Browne-key-job.html (2010).

This extreme position may surprise you, because, after all, corporate success must surely be driven by some sort of criterion besides pure randomness! And it is. But these criteria do not even remotely resemble the theoretical definition of "results" that economic forces, shareholders, or logical management theory would expect. According to these theories, "good results" would generally be defined as some combination of: increasing the value of the company; increasing profit; increasing customer satisfaction, retention, loyalty; increasing market share, brand perception, competitiveness; completing commissioned projects on time and on budget; deploying new products according to commissioned specifications; reducing costs, development time, errors; increasing employee morale; increasing employee retention; building cohesive teams that function as units; increasing productivity. Note that "results" do not include the simple completion of organisational processes or the mass production of strategies, which have zero value until their output is implemented (and measured); consider them only "steps" towards, but definitely not, per se, results.

Your company will invariably assign specific, measurable result targets to your cyclical performance reviews. Every enlightened organisation likes to tell itself (and its employees) that it is objective, results-oriented, and metrics-driven in evaluating employee performance and, eventually, in making promotion decisions. Do not believe it. You will be the rare employee if your manager even remembers the metrics you are supposed to be driving, let alone *how* to measure them.

During a final exit interview with the local managing director of one of my large, world-class corporate employers, I was asked for my biggest piece of advice. I told him to actively measure the performance and results of his teams. Did he know whether the teams had increased productivity? Did he know whether they were meeting their metrics? Did he even know what they were being measured on? I saw him squirm and his eyes glaze over as he contemplated the unfathomable difficulty of ever actually attempting to do such a thing. Six months later, the entire company reorganised (fully eliminating the need to actually measure results for teams that no longer existed!). The company continues to reorganise on average every eighteen months.

You may be wondering by now, if results don't matter, what does? Before this topic is addressed, it is important to explain precisely *why* results don't matter. Assume for the moment that a company is run by mediocre management (how this eventually invariably occurs is addressed later in this book). The most simple yet profound explanation is: **no one has time to measure results**. To be more accurate from a corporate perspective: no one prioritises highly enough the time/effort to measure results.

Probably the biggest contributors to this situation are modern standards of employment velocity. *It is extremely rare for any manager to spend more than one to two years in a single role.* The significance of this cycle cannot be overemphasised. If he is "bad" or otherwise not performing, he will usually leave the company within that time period for employment elsewhere. If he is "mediocre" or "good", he will either be promoted or "reorganised" to another role, or . . . he will invariably leave the company for employment elsewhere (more pay, more responsibility, and so forth). At levels below vice president, spending one to two years in a role and two to four years with any one company are pretty standard in most modern white-collar corporations. Take a random walk through LinkedIn to see for yourself. In my own career of fourteen years, I have had fifteen managers, of whom only eight resulted from my own initiative (changing departments or companies); the rest of my managers have come and gone as a result of leaving the company, being reassigned, moving, promotions, and so forth.

This short managerial tenure combines with the difficulty of measuring results to essentially make corporate commitment to results an exercise in smoke and mirrors. Often, results take a long time to surface. Decisions and actions taken today may not bear fruit for years. Deciding to change the product characteristic of your company's widget will take six months to get through product development, another three months to fully deploy to the marketplace, three months to market and to promote, and another six months to measure the impact of the new characteristic. A year and a half after the decision, the result of that decision *may* be known—*if* you are lucky. Results of truly significant and impactful decisions remain unknown for many years in cases such as going into new lines of business, launching new products with no previous history, establishing corporate culture policies, making hiring decisions, and so forth.

Moreover, most results, by their nature, are difficult to isolate in an impact analysis. With hundreds of changes (i.e., variables) being made to your company's product (pricing, product configuration, marketing message, PR positioning, competitor's reactions, and so forth), rather disciplined analytical and statistical approaches are needed to determine whether a particular decision correlates with (let alone causes) success. Doing this properly requires disciplined and accurate measurement, variable isolation, control groups, and, most importantly, time enough for the data to accumulate. I have worked in high-tech, world-class, progressive companies in which the best variable impact analysis processes are inferior in rigour to what you would find in a ninth-grade chemistry class. And these companies *prided* themselves on being metrics driven. Suffice it to say, the average corporation does not even merit mention regarding analytical rigour or disciplin.

Finally, attribution of results to previous roles becomes exponentially harder with each increment. If a manager knows that he will be out of his current role in a year; that in the next role, he will have a whole new host of objectives; and that no one will remember results from the old role, let alone his manager, who is probably a new one anyway and most likely moving on in a year as well, what incentive does this employee possibly have to care about results? None.

For fun, let us take a structured logic approach to the above thought process:

1. I am an employee X who started a new job at time t=0. I am given 3 months to ramp up and start producing decisions. I make a decision Y at time t=3 (months).

2. Given the nature of this decision, I think it may have measurable results in 12 months (at time t=15).

3. However, this is a difficult decision for which to isolate effects, so the measurement will only be 50% accurate anyway (i.e., saying the decision was positive or negative can be done with only 50% confidence). If it is negative, I can credibly argue that the measurement is incorrect.

4. If the effect is negative, I can also blame part of it on my predecessor, who is not around to contradict my arguments ("it turns out he left me with a wrong baseline, I had to clean up his mess, etc. etc.").

5. It is 60% likely that my manager will himself move on within the next 1 year to another role/job by time t=15. The new manager will not know anything about my predecessor nor even really about how the decision Y was made or what the reasons were at the time. I can make up any story I want.

6. It is 60% likely that I also will move on to a new role/job at time t=15, in which case, if I get promoted, I have no reason anymore to worry about decision Y (because I am already promoted!); if I leave the company, likewise (because no one in my new company will have access to metrics from my old company); and, if I move laterally, I can credibly claim that I was not really given a chance to finish putting Y in place, so, of course, it failed.

7. Finally, I know my manager is using the exact same logic process I am using, so I just have to make sure not to stick him with any directly attributable bad results in the next 12 months before either of us moves, and we will all get along fine.

Each item above is a "degree of freedom" that in combination multiply out (not add up) to make it exponentially more difficult to attribute results to an individual's performance. (A back-of-the-envelope calculation shows that the odds of my manager from time t=0 confronting me at time t=15 with the negative results of my decision and my being unable to argue my way out of it is only 8%). Moreover, Point 7 shows how this process "recurses" all up and down the organisation: if it is true for Employee X, it is true for his subordinates, manager, manager's manager, and so forth. With so many insurmountable degrees of freedom, the dirty little secret of corporations is that they do not really try to measure most results directly. Interestingly, the very flexibility and liquidity of the modern era's employment marketplace seems to have produced this negative consequence. In the old days, when employees stayed in roles for five years, the odds of the results of their decisions catching up with them were a lot greater. Now, the mediocre employee need not worry about that.

I once had an e-mail discussion with a senior vice president at a large world-class corporation who was soliciting feedback about how to improve on dismal employee survey results regarding managerial leadership in the department. I suggested tying evaluation of managerial performance to, for example, not only how many new employees were hired but how long they stayed at the company and how well they performed versus the company average. Of course, this would require tracking some metrics for several years and having those metrics "trail" a manager even to new roles in new departments. What might seem an obvious way to measure one aspect of managerial performance (i.e., the results-focused definition of "team building", one of the more important roles of senior management) is prohibitively difficult to the mediocre senior executive. Which is to say—not a single step in this direction has been taken at that company.

The world of global finance has already served as an example of failures to hold executives accountable for results. This should not be news, as even they are so acutely aware of the principles in this chapter that they have created an acronym to precisely remind each other with a wink and a nod of these inefficiencies whenever they contemplate doing a risky deal: **IBGYBG**. Screwing over the shareholders or investors or even their own companies will not pose a problem, because by the time the deal comes a cropper, "I'll Be Gone, You'll Be Gone".[5] While this strategy is often a direct result of calculated risks and returns, the mediocre employee can simply accept it as a general state of things in the corporate world and not bother himself too much with the math.

---

5   This phrase was brought into the light and the public's attention in *The Accidental Investment Banker* by Jonathan Knee (2006), as cited by Glyn Holton, "I'll Be Gone, You'll Be Gone," *The New Capitalist*, http://glynholton.com/2007/01/ill-be-gone-youll-be-gone/ (2007).

There are ways to overcome the cycle of short-termism in a corporation or a team. But, at a minimum, they require that a nonmediocre manager, a board of directors member, or even a shareholder break out of the recursive logic process shown above and *impose results accountability* on all those below (which is extremely rare in a corporation, as this book later outlines). For now, remember: millions of decisions are made in a company every day. The more complicated the decision, the more impact it has, the higher the level of responsibility it requires—the less results-driven it is.

👍 👍 👍

Important note: The only exception to the primary rule of this chapter is if you are in a Sales organisation. In this case, results are the *only* thing that matters. Invert all the content you have just read in this chapter, and focus on that. Do not worry about relationships, positioning, perception, and so forth—just deliver on your sales numbers, and try to exceed them. Sales organisations are set up to care about one thing and one thing only. If you work in a Sales organisation, you can skip reading Chapter 2.

CHAPTER 2
Perception Will Do

Understanding why results don't matter leads to the next topic: what *does* matter? And more importantly for you: how can the mediocre employee pursue what really does matter and thereby attain success? What does get measured in corporations? It is true that it is no longer acceptable to simply promote the tall, well-spoken, white, golf club buddy, alma-mater alum, or otherwise pleasant person, as so humorously depicted in the 1960s musical *How to Succeed in Business Without Really Trying* (which itself is based on a 1952 book by Shepherd Mead that might be considered the analogue to this one, albeit from two generations ago). These days, corporations like to use more defensible metrics, but instead of real results, they use soft results or result proxies.

What is important to remember about these is that they do not necessarily correlate to actual results, except in some qualitative abstraction. To use a simple illustration: rainfall is objectively measured by accumulated depth of rainwater in a container over a specified period of time ("5 inches of rain fell in a 24 hour period"). A corporation would instead typically use any one of the following to determine how much rain fell:

- Bob is one of our senior experienced guys, and he's usually pretty right, and he says it rained a lot today, and a lot means about 5 inches or so, from him.

- The weather today looked exactly like it did last Monday, and it rained about 5 inches then, so it probably rained about 5 inches today.

- When it rains all day, it accumulates 10 inches, but it only rained half a day, so that means it rained about 5 inches.

- If it rained more than 6 inches, we would have heard complaints from our customers and we didn't, and if it rained less that 4 inches we wouldn't have made our weekly target and we did, so that means it rained about 5 inches.

Now, note that none of the above is logically incorrect. Moreover, they are all relatively objective, and even somewhat relevant! Possibly, even true! The problem is: none of them actually *measures the result*. This is a perfect tactic for the mediocre to employ—use soft or proxy measurement of results that are hard to argue with and that can be qualitatively linked to the actual topic while requiring little effort to produce and leaving explanatory wiggle room if questioned. It is now time to be more rigorous and to itemise the things that *do* matter in a corporation.

The first and most important factor is **other people's comments**. More often than not, these are not the formal comments made in performance reviews or feedback sessions but **casual** gossip or hallway conversations. Usually, they are no more than a few short sentences. They may be occasioned by the manager's asking a peer, "So how is Nicole doing on that project to launch the new widget?" To which the manager from the other department will usually reply, "She's doing great; the team loves her and I think she has the right approach to get this thing done". Or, the reply will be, "I'm not sure she's the right person for the job; she didn't take some advice I gave her and she's pursuing an approach that Rob from Finance disagrees with." At this point, Nicole's manager will nod knowingly, having understood as much as he thinks is necessary, and ask about the next meeting with the departmental VP and whether the slide deck is ready to go.

This approach serves a brilliant double purpose for the mediocre manager: first of all, it makes him appear to be a team player who values advice and input from peers. The manager will also have a very defensible ally whose view corroborates his at the next promotion or salary review. There is nothing managers like less than going out on a limb for their employees and spending their own goodwill capital. Secondly, in an organisation where everyone has little time for actual analysis of results (Chapter 1's lesson), mediocre managers will just let someone else execute that "analysis" for them! Without actually asking for specifics, they will "trust" their peers to have made informed, objective decisions regarding Nicole's performance. As a matter of fact, the fewer specific details conveyed in the conversations, the better! Details may start to become fact-based and controvertible, requiring thinking and possibly work to investigate. So the ideal scenario for a mediocre manager is to have three or four other managers give one-to two-sentence generic evaluations of an employee, upon which all future decisions will be based. In the dozens of water cooler discussions I have had with people managers over the years, I can count on one hand the number of times these discussions lasted more than two minutes. (This approach to employee evaluation is analysed more in Chapter 3: Myths About the Performance Review.)

Knowing this, a mediocre employee must focus relentlessly on getting other managers at roughly the same or senior level to her own manager *to like her* and to have one to two positive things to say about her at all times. These things most definitely do not need to be results-based, as already explained, but can be about anything at all. *"She's very charismatic." "She has a go get 'em attitude." "She's very fast." "She did a great job organising our team dinner." "She's always the first with ideas at our team meetings."* Note that the recommended tactic that emerges here is to **instil a positive perception**, of almost any kind, in tangentially affiliated managers.

The mediocre employee will naturally wonder what the relationship with her own manager should be. Perhaps counter-intuitively, the answer is: as light as possible. Familiarity breeds contempt; knowledge breeds evaluation. Remember, you start out in a sort of honeymoon period: when you are hired, or even accepted into a new department, your manager thinks you are the best thing to come along in a while (which is why you have been put there). Your CV, flawless interviewing skills, and charismatic smile got you there. Almost anything you do afterwards can only reduce your appeal in the eyes of your manager. Moreover, if your manager actually knows what you are working on or the objectives you are achieving, he is likely to have opinions on the quality, performance, or results of these duties. More often than not, they will be negative opinions (having positive ones usually requires a nonmediocre manager, which is very rare in corporations, something that is addressed later in this book).

So, stay away! **Avoid your manager as much as possible.** Do not manifestly hide from him, but do not purposefully seek him out for extended interactions. Do not engage in lengthy debates, do not present complex analysis, try not to co-work on projects. As a mediocre employee, your ideal scenario is to have your manager have a faint idea that you are good and capable and to receive a lot of lightweight feedback from other managers (as described above). Remember, it is a lot harder to make yourself look good in the eyes of a mediocre manager than to make yourself look bad. So, try not to make yourself look anything.

However, should you have more exposure to your manager than you would prefer, there are ways to improve his perception of you as well. (These techniques also handily apply to tangential managers who will later give casual feedback on you, as described above). First: *look busy.* Always be running to meetings, talking seriously with people in the hallways, and having difficulty scheduling time in your calendar. Be working on as many projects simultaneously as you can assign yourself to. Take full advantage of the *action bias*[6] that insidiously pervades almost all corporations.

On this topic, one very important tip: the perception of you if you say, "no, I am too busy to work on project X" is much more negative than if you *accept the project and later say*, "sorry, I have been too busy working on these five

---

6   The *action bias* is the desire to do something rather than nothing when the status quo of a situation is not acceptable (which in corporations it never is—growth is perpetually mandatory). The action bias was notably explored in a study by Offer H. Azar, et al. ("Action bias among elite soccer goalkeepers: The case of penalty kicks," *MPRA*, http://mpra.ub.uni-muenchen.de/4477/ (2005)) that showed that goalkeepers tend to jump to one side or another during a penalty kick, even though they would be better off statistically by staying put. But, fans expect them to do *something*, not just stand there, and goalies comply, with the result of much poorer performance. The action bias is further explored in the economic sphere in Patricia Cohen's article "The Art of the Save, for Goalie and Investor," *The New York Times*, http://www.nytimes.com/2008/03/01/business/01kick.html (2008).

other important projects at the request of my manager to get to project X". Moreover, it is quite possible that either priorities change or you or the requestor moves elsewhere, so chances are good that the project would never need to be done anyway. The amount of effort required to execute either answer is identical—none. So stick with the answer that leaves the better impression of you. The requestor will have no choice but to take your word for the fact that the other five projects your manager gave you were more important and, moreover, will even think more highly of you because you were trusted with projects much more important than project X that he offered you. For him to think anything else, he would have to actually go to your manager, ask about the five projects, describe project X, have a debate as to which project was more important, and so forth. You can count on this never happening. **Always accept all offered projects**, and blow off the ones you do not actually want to work on. (This rule applies to anyone asking you for something *except* your direct manager; when to accept projects from your manager is dealt with below.)

In a corporation, you should actively help yourself **look busy by volunteering** for various committees, special groups, tiger teams, and so forth. More often than not, they are secondary to the primary business of the corporation (which is why the primary organisational structure is not being used), so results expected of them are even more abstract (unless it is party planning; do not volunteer for these projects, because they are definitely not worth the effort). At the same time, by volunteering for various optional team projects, you project the appearance of caring for the organisation and being multitalented, committed to cross-functional efforts, and proactive. Typically, these projects require little work but have elevated executive sponsor profiles, helping you look good to the managers whose bright idea these committees were. Such group projects typically are things like work-life balance committees, employee satisfaction improvement task forces, corporate mission statement/beliefs tiger teams, job description formalisation workgroups, and of course party planning. (Stay away! Your colleagues will love you, but only if the party goes unusually well, while senior managers will be indifferent because they never really show up [see Chapter 4]. On the other hand, if it goes poorly, *everyone* will dislike you.)

It also helps to **be scarce or difficult to find.** Lack of availability implies that you are very busy, which implies that you are doing important things, which implies that you are a really good worker. Of course, never put yourself in a position where you cannot be found if necessary (slipping off to the golf course in the middle of the day is only for senior VPs and above), but do not feel as though you have to be at your desk all day; you are mediocre, not lazy! Besides appearing at many company meetings, engage in a lot of (real) offsite meetings with partners, providers, vendors, and so forth. This technique is extra effective, because your manager will never actually call them to find out what you talked about and will not be able to get any "water cooler" feedback about you, allowing you to completely write your own story. Be choppy about answering e-mails or even phone calls. Wait a day sometimes to answer e-mail messages, even from your manager. Again, most of the time, the first reaction from the outreaching party is "She must be really busy", rather than "She is probably shirking again." Just do not do anything that can actually get you fired! Stay within the corporate rules.

Scarcity can be an extremely elegant method for the mediocre employee when played off against multiple managers. The stratagem works as follows: assume you can convince your manager that your project requires you to work closely with another group for a period of two weeks—so closely that you actually have to be located there (even better if the location is several time zones away). The most that your manager will do will be to send a letter to the manager of the other group saying, "I need Robert to work on project X, and I'd like him to work closely with your team. Thanks." Your manager is very busy and will not be too precise about the details. Now, you arrive at the remote team, but that manager has no idea how much of your time you are supposed to devote to that project, only that your manager trusts you enough to send you (so you must be good). You can spend half your time working on project Y for some other manager, who is just glad to have an unexpected extra pair of hands. Meanwhile, your manager has no idea what you are doing because you are quite far away, and, because travel is expensive, you do not need to answer his other inquiries because you are very busy working on project X! Moreover, you can tell this manager of project X that your manager also expected you to work on project Y 75 percent of the time, so the 50 percent project X is getting is actually extra effort you are putting in. At the end of the day: the manager of project X is glad for your extra effort and sends a great thank you note after two weeks, the manager of project Y is glad to have had extra help and sends a great thank you note too, and your own manager, not actually having seen what you worked on or even having received answers to his other queries but having just received two good reviews for you, thinks you must be good and must have been working on important things and makes a mental note of it. The key to this method is lack of information imposed through your own scarcity. *If you are not around, no one can ask you or see what you are doing; they will by default assume it is something useful.* The same mechanism can be used on a microscale within the same large office; travel is not specifically required.

At some companies I have known, the employees of whole departments have built their entire careers on this model: move around a lot, talk to many different people, have many meetings as frequently as possible, do small favours for each colleague, and watch the 'thank you's add up to promotions (such departments are often inclined to have names like as Business Development, Strategic Partnerships, or HR).

A special case of applied scarcity comes up in companies that heavily employ the modern technology of e-mail and instant messaging. **Truly busy and important people may take many days to respond to an e-mail, if at all, and hardly ever use instant messaging.** Mediocre employees absolutely *must* mimic this strategy, even if artificially. As a rule, *never* respond to e-mails right away; hold off until the end of the day or, even better, stretch it out to two or three days (provided no hard deadline is attached). Every once in a while, you should even ignore an e-mail entirely (you will find that this approach is not as painful as it sounds: a very good rule of thumb in the corporate world is that *if you wait long enough, problems go away on their own*). For an instant message, wait ten to fifteen minutes to respond if it is from a senior manager; otherwise, feel free to ignore it entirely—the sender can e-mail you if the topic is important enough. If the message is from your manager, also wait to respond, unless you know that he knows that you are at your computer. Not only will delaying your responses make you look as though you are busy doing real, important work, but it will also give you extra time to chart your course as a mediocre employee, instead of spending all day replying to e-mails and chats.

For the mediocre employee, the imperative to look busy extends not just to your actions but also your mouth. Which is to say, **talk a lot.** Already suggested as a method for looking busy by way of hallway conversations, talking is also especially important in meetings as a way to instil in your colleagues the perception that you are engaged, possibly intelligent, and probably right about something. Do not blurt out obvious inanity; you are mediocre, not stupid! Use your brain to talk about the subject at hand, to come up with instant relevant ideas, to show great enthusiasm, and to otherwise make it known that you are *present*. Do not make the mistake of thinking that a well-considered, well-thought-out comment has much value (the value may indeed be there, but only much later, when everyone has forgotten the meeting and who said what). *Thoughtfulness* is easily confused with *thoughtlessness* or laziness, because they have the same outward manifestations (i.e., silence!). Mark Twain's dictum "Better to keep your mouth shut and appear ignorant than open it and remove all doubt" is completely *reversed* in the corporate world: "Better to open your mouth and risk being ignorant then keep it shut and appear to be so." Talking in meetings is an essential but cheap (because you do not actually have to do any work) way of building your reputation in a corporation. Call it **personal PR propaganda**.[7]

At one self-respecting company where I worked, I knew a manager who had built an entire career on blurting out earnest semi-nonsense at various team meetings and high-profile events, such as, "I'm *really so glad* to be here working with all of you"; "This project is *really important* and will be great for the customer"; "Let's have a meeting with these three other stakeholders to discuss how to make this fantastic idea happen." It is true that most of us opened our eyes wide with stupefaction every time she opened her mouth, but

---

7   "The difference between [Public Relations] (i.e. PR) and propaganda is that the former tries to shape the truth while the latter seeks to subvert it" (ThoughtEchoes, Twitter, http://twitter.com/thoughtechoes/status/19246950747 (2010)). If you are mediocre, you will definitely need to subvert that fact and substitute for it the appearance of excellence.

she was just too energetic and enthusiastic for the company management to do anything but promote her several times. She certainly was never seen doing any work. For the above-average mediocre employee, though, the more diverse your commentary and the more relevant to the subject, the better you will be perceived. Start practicing right away.

Another useful method to employ, and one of classic and enduring utility, is to **be the hero**. Handling apparent crises or emergency situations looks good! (Regardless of who caused them or whether they are even true emergencies.) Even when you have everything under control, do not show it. Again, much more important is the *perception of doing difficult or critical work* rather than the true difficulty of the work done (which few of your colleagues will know and even fewer will measure). Always look like you are under pressure, always look like you are working to tight deadlines and exerting yourself, always project that the success of the project depends on you. Sun Tzu, the great ancient Chinese general, once observed, "For to win one hundred victories in one hundred battles is not the acme of skill. To subdue the enemy without fighting is the acme of skill."[8] The mediocre employee will never forget that this lesson is *poorly internalised by corporations* and ripe for exploit and will seek to be perceived as a winner of battles. You do not get the Congressional Medal of Honor for diplomacy.

You can even manufacture your own "battles" to make yourself a hero. This principally relies on the natural tendency of managers to not be too inquisitive about a project when it seems to be going well or things are quiet. They usually only worry about deadlines, output, costs, and so forth when a problem surfaces or a crisis is imminent. So, during the early period of low oversight (which is usually

---

8   Sun Tzu, as quoted in "Sun Tzu," *Wikipedia*, http://en.wikiquote.org/wiki/Sun_Tzu (2011).

about 80 percent of the project's life, actually), **create your own problems that need hero fixes**. First, because they will be problems of your own making, you will know how to fix them. Moreover, you can use the time and energy that you saved up front ignoring the emergence of the problem and simply allocate them to the later period to fix the same problem. Being a hero can actually be managed not to require any more effort than regular work! The pivotal thing to remember: no one knows you actually caused the problem to start with.

On one project I was managing, my team and I had to work the weekend to ensure it was complete. It was a pretty intense weekend, and on Monday morning, my manager was full of ebullient praise for my hard work and even offered me some reward and public recognition. At the time, I had to explain to her that she really should not be thanking me for working the weekend, because this six-month project had provided us all ample time to do everything well before the final weekend. However, if she actually *wanted* me to work more emergency weekends, that could easily be arranged. If I had not pointed this out, perhaps I could have profited from many more manufactured weekends of heroism.

Up to this point in this chapter, the recommendations and tactics have been essentially context-independent, relying solely on the directed effort of the mediocre employee to execute them. They can be done in any organisation, in any department, on any project, at any time. However, several other complex issues that are of great importance to the success of a mediocre employee require actions based on the specifics of the situation. These are the so-called "traditional" steps to success about which many books (and *Dilbert* comic strips) have been written. Rather than give case-by-case specifics, this book will limit itself to the general direction that should be pursued on each topic.

Do everything in your power to work on high-profile projects. It is not sufficient to have the appearance of success on regular projects; if you wish to succeed in a corporation, it is essential that these be *high-profile* ones. How do you know if a project is high-profile? Here is one easy heuristic: every modern company has "awards" or other forms of public recognition of what it considers to be good work. It becomes abundantly clear as a project gathers steam whether it is a good candidate for such an award. If you see one . . . join it ASAP! Other essential characteristics of a high-profile project include: more than one executive sponsor (that is how you know it is not one person's pet project); short or mid-term project duration, preferably fewer than nine months (longer projects have a huge risk of losing managerial interest as people and priorities change); the goal of expanding the business, scope, or headcount of a corporation, such as new lines of business or mergers/acquisitions (new is always perceived as good; by the time the sheen fades, you will be long gone); and involvement of many departments within the organisation (sponsoring managers will ensure the project appears successful, because their own corporate reputations will also depend on it). By working on high-profile projects, you create the visibility and then the perception of drive and momentum that you need to succeed in the organisation.

If you are not working on at least several high-profile projects, you should take the drastic step of simply refusing to do anything else. Yes, this extreme approach should be employed by the mediocre employee, despite what managers, the corporation, or even a sense of obligation may dictate. The simple fact is: your insubordination *may possibly* cost you goodwill from your managers, but not working on high-profile projects is *guaranteed* to limit your success. It is that simple. Your situational context may even help you minimize the damage from your outright refusal: you may still be in your posthiring honeymoon period with residual goodwill; you may be a good talker and find reasons to explain why you could not possibly work on the project proposed; you may be able to skilfully employ the scarcity manoeuvre (see above). But once you are on a high-profile project, all your sins will be long forgotten as the project barrels towards the corporate award for excellence.

And what book on organisational behaviour would be complete without the eternal truism: **make your boss look good**. Yes, this is most definitely required, even for the mediocre. What makes this task challenging is that every boss has a different way of functioning and different needs, and finding ways to make her look good must be done while simultaneously following the rules discussed above. What you must do is find out your manager's priorities, find out what would make her look good in front of her manager as well as the rest of the organisation, and then support all of those—but only to the extent that the work is high-profile, can make you look like a hero, gives you the opportunity to do a lot of talking, and, of course, does not require you to spend too much time working directly with your manager. If your manager does not disseminate her written objectives, then you should talk to her peers and to her manager, and do a lot of listening to her; priorities emerge very quickly in just a few conversations.

👍 👍 👍

Let us use a few examples to illustrate the mental heuristics about how to correctly choose projects that make your boss look good.

Case 1: Your manager comes to you and says, "Joe, my boss, Bob, asked me the other day at our one-on-one to take a look at cutting our printing costs. I'd like you to take a look at it." What do you answer?

Case 2: Your manager asks you to work on thirty-person project with one big deliverable in eighteen months. How do you respond?

Case 3: You notice that your manager talks a lot at meetings about growing revenue stream. What do you do?

Here are the correct responses for a mediocre employee:

Case 1: Under no circumstances should you accept this project. For all of the following reasons: it is a pet project only of Bob's; it is not really a priority for your manager (as of yet); it is a back-office task with little visibility and low cross-functional exposure. Outright refuse it. (Your excuse will heavily depend on the circumstances: there is no single approach.)

Case 2: This is a questionable project to be involved in: it is doubtful that whatever the priority of this project is will still be the priority in eighteen months or that you or your manager will be around to reap the rewards. It will be difficult for you to be a frequent hero, given that the project has only one big deliverable at the end. On the upside: this is a big project with many people, which will give you ample opportunity to talk a lot as well as many chances to make yourself scarce or to even join busy-looking subcommittees. You should see if you can join the project, but identify which part of it your manager values most and try to carve out that part for yourself. Definitely to do not plan on staying on the project until the end, but envision transitioning off in at most six months.

Case 3: A new revenue stream is an obvious priority for your manager, and it involves something new. Offer to create a special team designed to plan a new product offering (indeed, tell your manager you have already spoken to several important people about it and they think it is a good idea; he will never check anyway). Make sure this is a very cross-functional team with as many managers as you can get to put a stake into the plan. Talk a lot in the meetings to show how committed and driven you are. Define the key deliverable to be a big PowerPoint presentation, and wait until the last week to do it; at which point, summon all-hands on deck and work several late nights to get it out just in time. Make sure you get recognised as the hero for pulling it together at the last minute, but be sure to thank your manager as the sponsor of the project and the one who inspired you to undertake it. (As for whether the presentation actually makes a good case for the new revenue stream or whether the new revenue stream actually ever materialises—well, by now, the mediocre employee knows that this does not matter much.)

As mentioned before, making your boss look good is very context-dependent, so you will have to be very observant and careful in planning your steps and communicating your approach if you truly wish to avoid doing a lot of meaningless work and maximising your chances of corporate success. But with such an approach, the mediocre can succeed in a corporation even more rapidly than the excellent.

CHAPTER 3
Myths About the Performance Review

At this point, it is worth focusing on a specific artefact of the modern corporation: the performance review process. Having established that results don't matter but perceptions do, what is consequently the role of this seemingly appropriately and reassuringly named activity in a modern corporation?

As smaller companies grow, they find that they need to institute formal review processes to try to manage the complexity, fluidity, and legal requirements of large human resource organisations. These typically take the shape of official annual, semi-annual, or sometimes quarterly cycles of verbal and written feedback, usually culminating in a single document summarising this feedback and further recommendations from your manager. Employees will be asked to participate by writing self-feedback and possibly peer reviews. Managers will be obligated to give feedback to all their reports. This body of content is ostensibly then used during the promotion, salary, and bonus decision-making processes.[9] You should be aware of several very popular myths about the performance review if you truly wish to be successful as a mediocre employee. The bigger and older the company, the more mythical these are.

Myth 1: What is written matters. Your written performance review will only reflect what your manager is willing to commit to paper to avoid legal liability or direct confrontation (for example, if your manager at some point thinks she will need to fire you, most companies require that poor performance be well-documented during recent performance reviews; likewise, if the manager writes too little, she may be challenged by you or HR for not completing the formality). What your manager *really* thinks about you, she will highlight to you verbally . . . or not at all. She knows that no one will ever actually look at the written feedback unless she chooses to show it to someone (i.e., by nominating you for promotion . . . or for dismissal), and, if this is the case, she will have a much broader platform in which to explain her true thoughts, anyway.

Consequently, the mediocre employee will learn very quickly not to worry about the syntax *or even the content* of the written performance review. If you disagree with any of it, do not bother to get it changed, either. Doing so will just irritate your manager, without yielding any benefit.

---

9   Some companies try to buck the trend. Atlassian, a globally successful Australian software company, realised early on in its corporate lifetime that the traditional methods are broken. It is attempting to define a different model of performance review based on its employees' needs. This exception to the typical way of doing things proves the rule that companies overwhelmingly simply adopt existing, broken approaches by default (so unusual is it to not be a slave to custom that even *Fortune* magazine has written about Atlassian's experiment: Polly LaBarre, "Giving the performance review an extreme makeover," *Fortune*, http://management.fortune.cnn.com/2011/02/16/giving-the-performance-review-an-extreme-makeover/ (2011)). However, as a mediocre employee, you will never be hired by Atlassian, so you can safely expect to always be subject to the traditional performance review model described above.

Remember from earlier chapters that perception is what matters, and the type of perception that matters is usually not the kind to be written down in formal reviews, where logic and justification are required. Besides, *no one* will ever actually read the text of your review ever again (see below).

Myth 2: Feedback from your *peers* has an impact. This has become extremely trendy in enlightened performance processes (buzzword: "360-degree feedback"), because it purports to balance the single viewpoint of an employee's manager with other viewpoints and to give the manager more information for his own appraisal. But the fact is, it will not be *your* peers from whom your manager takes counsel (many, if not most of whom will be mediocre in their own rights!); it will be from *his peers, or superiors.* And these will be, by definition, other managers more senior than you. Your manager will in no case let the opinions of a bunch of people at your level supersede the opinions of a few people at his level and above. The filing cabinets of corporations are littered with the resignation letters of managers who take a bullet for their subordinates by disagreeing with senior management.

Thus, the mediocre employee should waste no time soliciting feedback from peers but should focus specifically on a few high-profile managers whom his own manager respects and listens to. And remember, as explained earlier, those opinion-forming exchanges will have already occurred at the water cooler, long before the performance review process takes place. So, nominate only high-profile managers who *perceive you* as a good employee and will give you good written feedback, if only so their own credibility is boosted should you get promoted or at some point even become their peer.

I once asked about fifteen of my colleagues to give me feedback during a regular review cycle. I had been working with many cross-functional teams and geographies and actually really wanted to know what they thought, as it was early in my tenure. The way the process was set up, my manager was able to see online who my nominated reviewers were. He e-mailed me and told me to reduce the number of reviewers to five. I was quite surprised, because I did not expect him to be so blunt about his lack of interest but rather to just passively ignore what he did not wish to read, as is customary. I did not change a thing; if he was not going to read all the feedback, at least I would.

Myth 3: Managers wait until they read feedback before deciding their positions/opinions. Given that peer feedback is irrelevant and that the perceptions of other senior managers have already been conveyed at the water cooler long before, there is really no need to read anything at all from the performance review, is there? This includes your own feedback on yourself, which is shown below to be irrelevant. Besides, it would be a truly useless manager who did not already know how his employee was performing far, far in advance of the completion of the usually protracted yet always rushed written performance review process.

Amazingly, at one company I worked for that prided itself on engineering excellence (which requires avoiding scheduling deadlock conditions), perpetual adjustments were made to the sequence of the performance review steps, which at one point led to an explicit deadline for the managers to finish their own written performance reviews and to submit their ratings *before* the "peer feedback" was due for completion. Even though everyone knew how the game was played anyway, the blatant hypocritical absurdity of this caused a few voices to be raised and for HR to tweak the timeline . . . and give precisely *one day* beyond the written feedback deadline for the managers to complete their own submissions. Even the mediocre reader will accurately guess how much of the written peer feedback was actually read by managers. (The submediocre reader, if there are any, does need this spelled out: none of it was read.) I never cease to be amazed at how little feedback other managers solicit from me during the performance review process about their employees with whom I have worked for a long time. The fact is, they have already made up their minds a long time ago.

Myth 4: A good review is sufficient to succeed. Remember that a good review may only appear so simply because the manager does not want to commit anything negative to paper or just does not have time to bother. The manager knows that the review itself does not matter (Myth 1!). Moreover, it is in the company's interest to inflate review ratings to motivate employees for as long as possible without actually promoting them, which is why you will find that corporations typically have some sort of targets for an "above average" rating for 40 percent of all employees but promotion rates of only 10 percent per year or so, for example. Statistically, by the way, that works out to being promoted on average once every four years for someone who is *consistently exceeding expectations.* This may not be enough for the ambitious mediocre employee, such as the reader.

Companies will also try to position good reviews as rewards in and of themselves. This approach comes from perverting the theories of management psychology, which find that for some people, praise, recognition, and so forth can be rewards in their own right, so companies will grant good reviews in lieu of raises or promotions: *"We think you are doing a great job, but we're not going to give you a raise (of anything but token significance). Instead, we will tell you emphatically that you're doing a great job and we value you highly. Carry on."* So goes the virtual argument (known as getting "grin-fucked"). However, the reader will have remembered that, in this book, success is defined in terms of raises and promotions. The mediocre employee who wishes to succeed will not let his manager fool him into accepting something of no intrinsic value. You should always insist that good reviews be accompanied by good rewards.

Myth 5: Self-reviews should be objective, including being self-critical. There is simply no reason to do this. Conscientious employees may think that something is to be gained from this approach and that the manager will value and respect objectivity and self-criticism and consequently increase the overall rating. Only if your manager is a saint or is retiring soon might this be true. The mediocre employee will never fall into this trap, even when the company tries to encourage it. Just as in an interview, where you *always* describe yourself in as perfect a light as you can, including embellishments and ideal framing, so, too, in each review cycle should you avoid bringing negatives to the attention of your manager (and possibly the promotion committee) and instead take as much credit for positives as you can talk your way into.

Negative things from your self-review will just be used by your manager to justify his own criticism, or, for that matter, might inform him of negatives he had overlooked. The likely downside for you of putting them on paper is much greater than the minuscule upside. As for positive things, try not to introduce any new ones on your review that you have not already brought to your manager's attention, lest they be disbelieved (your manager will think, "How come I don't know about this already if it's so important?").

Earlier in my career, I once wrote an objective evaluation of myself for a periodic review. In it, I described a rather successful project I had delivered (positive) but how I had had to push it through forcefully rather than gain consensus from another manager (negative). Despite the fact that the positive work on the project had taken several months and the negative "lack of consensus" with the other manager was an ethereal side effect with no consequence to the company or to anyone else, my manager was just looking for something to pounce on to knock my rating down to the next level. She needed to meet her "bell curve" ranking distribution requirements for the team,[10] and any excuse to bash my rating down was a good one.

Myth 6: Your review becomes part of your permanent record. If in the sense that it sits in some "filing cabinet"– yes, that is true. If, however, in the sense that anyone will ever look at it again–then no, this is a myth. Once the immediate performance cycle and the corresponding promotion cycle are complete, your review will never be of interest to anyone. Your current manager will not reference it because, his opinion having already been made, he will only lightly adjust it from his mental baseline in subsequent reviews. Future managers in the same company will be too busy integrating you into their teams or taking on their new management roles and too proud to let someone else prejudice their own expert evaluations of you. Why spend hours reading your legacy reviews (old news!) when they are so brilliant that they can formulate their own opinions after talking to you for ten minutes? And once you change companies, your old employer is legally required to keep your reviews confidential, so the reviews are in filing limbo forevermore. I have had fifteen managers to date in my career, and not

---

10   Human Resources had dictated that all teams without exception needed to have an internal ranking distribution of 10 percent "significantly exceeded expectations", 30 percent "exceeded expectations", 40 percent "met expectations", and 10 percent "did not meet expectations". My team had six people in it at the time, and my manager was forced to apply the ranking. There was not room for a third person to be exceeding expectations. See Chapter 6 on my very special thoughts about HR.

one of them has ever looked at a previous review, even after internal transfers or when they took over from my previous managers. This became evident in every case as they never referenced my history, knew little about my capabilities or deficiencies, and always wanted to reinvent my personal development plan from scratch. So, do not worry about your "permanent record": institutional memory is particularly short for performance reviews.

Ultimate Myth: The performance review process is an integral part of the accountability and decision making of your corporation. It is not: it is there for legal compliance/problem avoidance, because HR needs to feel important and useful, and to make employees believe that performance reviews and company rewards are objective and evidence-based. The mediocre employee will remember this, will let the Myths described in this chapter keep her from being needlessly distracted by the formal performance review cycle's smoke and mirrors, and will instead focus on the things that really do impact the way she is perceived and rated—namely, the subjective perceptions managers have already acquired long before (see Chapter 2).

The effectiveness of the performance review process itself would take so long to evaluate and to rate that the odds of a corporation having done this are nil. It would take hundreds of employees quitting before a CEO might realise something is wrong. This information would take years and years to accumulate (and to filter up past the self-justifying and obfuscating HR department). By which time, any CEO who may have started out caring would likely be long gone (with average tenure at an American corporation being 6.6 years[11]). And so,

---

11   Joan S. Lublin, "CEO Tenure, Stock Gains Often Go Hand-in-Hand," *The Wall Street Journal*, http://online.wsj.com/article/SB1000142405274870390000 4575325172681419254.html (2010).

the performance review process remains unaccountable and perpetually unoptimised.[12]

A final anecdote: On one occasion, my team at a large corporation with a very involved and comprehensive written quarterly review cycle had received no promotions during a

---

12   A few leading edge practitioners are starting to take note and research and write about the major problems with current approaches to performance reviews. However, they are at the fringes of their field. This *New York Times* article has a good overview: Tara Parker-Pope, "Time to eview Workplace Reviews?" *The New York Times*, http://well.blogs.nytimes.com/2010/05/17/time-to-review-workplace-reviews/ (2010). Here is an appropriate quote from Chapter 1 of the book referenced there, *Get Rid of the Performance Review!* (2010, ISBN 9780446556057), by Samuel A. Culbert, professor at UCLA's Anderson School of Management:

"This corporate sham is one of the most insidious, most damaging, and yet most ubiquitous of corporate activities. Everybody does it, and almost everyone who's evaluated hates it. It's a pretentious, bogus practice that produces absolutely nothing that any thinking executive should call a corporate plus. . . . "In fact, if firms did nothing else but just kill off this process they'd immediately be better off. When it comes to performance reviews, there's no question that nothing is better than something. That's how bad they are. The mission of this book is to put corporate executives on notice that they have created a monster. With the help of performance reviews, they've built a corporate culture where bullshit, not straight talk, is the communication etiquette of choice. . . .

"The performance review is the primary tool for reinforcing this sorry state. Performance reviews instil feelings of being dominated. They send employees the message that the boss's opinion of their performance is the key determinant of pay, assignment, and career progress. And while that opinion pretends to be objective, it is no such thing. The overriding message is that the boss's assessment is really about whether the boss 'likes' you, whether he or she feels 'comfortable' with you. None of this is good for the company unless the boss is some kind of savant genius and reads the employee with laser accuracy in understanding that person's inner talents and personal priorities to accurately choreograph his or her efforts. Unlikely.

"Put it another way: The performance review is the device that allows managers who do not understand human nature well enough to get along with the people they are charged with directing. It allows managers to avoid accountability for their misdeeds, incorrect opinions, and lack of knowledge. It is the insurance policy that allows managers to operate comfortably while employees are insecure. It is the tool that lets bosses be totally insensitive—and not worry about it."

yearly promotion review. They selected me to be the official liaison to the process administrator to find out why and on what basis other people in other teams got promotions. What were their accomplishments and achievements, I asked? The administrator, who had herself been promoted to director in that cycle, looked at me incredulously and promised to "raise the question" with management. I'm sure it still remains there, raised, at the top of their priority list, many years on. Just two years later, incidentally, that same person was promoted to a vice-president level in a performance review cycle for the entire duration of which she was out on maternity leave. We all wondered what magic words her official performance review must have contained for that year. But, because such files are confidential, no one will ever know!

CHAPTER 4
Familiarity Breeds Contempt

You surely have heard this trope before, and it is completely true in the corporate world—familiarity breeds contempt. Whereas your friends are self-selected (people who do not like you simply never become your friends), most of your work colleagues interact with you by force of circumstance. So they have just as much chance as a random person to become your friend. Assume you normally befriend 1 percent of the people you meet (which makes you already quite charming!). But with average odds of successful friendship that low, why would you try to befriend your co-workers?

The mediocre employee knows: do not try to become friends with co-workers. Do not appear sympathetic, do not share your personal problems with them, do not be cute, do not try to ingratiate yourself by listening to them whine for hours and giving your opinion, do not tell them about your wild partying youth, and do not invite them to your wedding. Under no circumstance let them become your

Facebook friends (whereas LinkedIn is actually a perfect way to connect because of its lack of personality).

The simple reason for this is human psychology. Most people in Western culture simply do not like most other people (math dictates that if you did, you would be friends with more than half the people you meet). And the more people get to know each others' weaknesses, foibles, and negative qualities, the more they dislike each other. Friendship and intimate knowledge, by nature, involves progressively revealing your weaknesses and negative qualities. Your real friends already like you and are sympathetic to you and will use these traits to make the friendship stronger, whereas co-workers will always look for excuses to categorise you as less qualified, less capable, less intelligent, or less worthy of advancement than they consider themselves. Do not give them any reasons to do so! As already discussed, perception is all-important, so keep their perceptions as high as they were the day they read your impressive, word-perfect résumé and the day you stepped through your office door for the first time, perfectly dressed, smiling, and, as far as they knew, infallible.

However, the mediocre employee will also understand that the true path lies not in being a stand-offish jerk and pissing off all your co-workers, but rather in **being *interesting*, without being familiar**. It is as much an error to disengage yourself completely from the opinions and discussions colleagues have about you as it is to overwhelm them with your gregarious nature. You need to actively shape the message, and it is best to shape it with positive impressions.

What are some ways to be interesting without being familiar? The best way is to engage co-workers in conversation about things that are unique or different about you but do not really tell them all that much about your personality, character, or preferences. Tell them about your exotic holiday (take some, even if only to have something to talk about at work!). Talk to them about your cool hobbies: motorcycle riding, any extreme sports, ballroom dancing, marathon running, rebuilding vintage cars, airplane piloting. It is okay even if the hobby is long in your past; it is *not* okay if the hobby is simply acquiring expensive things, such as vintage whiskey. If you have experienced a long period doing something "different", this makes great conversation: any military service, backpacking through the Andes, climbing Mount Everest, volunteering in the Peace Corps, getting a Ph.D.—such activities are generally impressive to everyone. If you come from someplace exotic (or small), such as Ireland, Madagascar, or Tahiti, you can talk at fantastic length about these places and keep people interested. If you happen upon someone knowledgeable in a sport that you know well, you will therein also have an endlessly fruitful topic of discussion that will permit you to exhibit as much fascinating knowledge and insight as you care to gain outside working hours.

But do not talk about things at which you have tried but failed: failed businesses, major accidents, getting fired. And do not talk about unglamorous (a.k.a. boring) hobbies: coin collecting, bird watching, landscaping, yoga. Do not talk about famous friends or relatives, because this connection instantly brings up the question of whether you have gotten where you are with their help. Do not talk about your past careers, because it is automatically implied that you failed at them (unless it is a glamorous career, such as being a combat veteran or supermodel). Weird habits or phobias, such as snoring, vertigo, or body piercing, are just not *interesting*, even if you feel that others might share them. Do not talk about periods of sickness or unemployment.

These might evoke sympathy, but sympathy in the office is a poison cloud that steadily transmogrifies into disdain. A good rule of thumb is that if at least 75 percent of your work colleagues would not say, "Wow, that's really interesting!" about a topic, do not talk about it.

Spending time with your colleagues while sharing interesting or exotic things about yourself is a great way to raise you in their esteem with a *triple* punch:

a) Conversation with anyone gives them the feeling that you are interested in them and their thoughts, making them like you more.

b) At the same time, you are feeding them positive, impressive, and distributable information about yourself that raises you in their esteem.

c) You are simultaneously preventing them from spending that time talking about how great they themselves are, which keeps their egos from growing.

The mediocre employee should not neglect to spend as much time doing this as possible and will always have some interesting topics of conversation ready for lunchtime, the water cooler, or after-work drinks.

Another extremely effective way to be interesting to your colleagues requires even less effort or a history of actually *doing* interesting stuff—**be funny**. In the office environment, humour is an almost universally prized quality that can be used to great effect. The psychological reasons why it is endearing and brings people together have been addressed in countless other books, but for the purpose of this one, it should be pointed out that one of its major benefits is that it, too, need not reveal anything personal about the speaker.

Being funny does require a certain talent, but it is a great way to engage your colleagues in talk, to raise their spirits, raise their esteem of you (*"he's such a funny guy!"*), and to not actually leave them knowing anything more about you than before. If you have any capability at all to be funny, practice it and use it as much as possible at work. Do not overdo it: do *not* become the office clown. At all costs, *avoid humour at your own expense* (this will negate the entire benefit!): do not put yourself down, do not joke about the quality of your own work, avoid funny stories from your personal past, do not make yourself seem inferior. Telling abstract jokes, joshing about someone else, relating workplace anecdotes, injecting a funny turn of a phrase—these, conversely, are all golden eggs that your golden goose mouth can keep laying and laying indefinitely.

There is yet another way to seem engaged with your colleagues without actually telling them anything. This way, however, is the way of the ultimate conversation master and is an extremely difficult and precise technique to execute. It is the equivalent of conversational jiu-jitsu, and I have seen it successfully executed only by the most accomplished senior managers who are perhaps in the upper echelons of the mediocre.

The technique work as follows. When you see a colleague, ask him how he is doing, and then ask him what's new or how the weekend went or even something more specific you know about. Then, as the colleague relates the story, you must say nothing, give no sign of approbation, or otherwise react. Maintain eye contact and attention, but nothing more—no nodding, no smiling. When the speaker is finished, immediately and distinctly move on to another topic (preferably something work-related).

What makes this technique so difficult is that it requires extreme control to not interject, co-involve, or otherwise participate in the monologue of the teller. Our natural reaction is to ingratiate ourselves using comments, laughs, or other marks of sympathy and understanding. Here is where the power of the proposed technique lies: by doing none of these, you put the speaker in a slightly awkward position of having said much without getting the cues of approval that he would normally expect. You have listened to the speaker, and the speaker is somewhat grateful, yet, at the same time, feels diminished relative to you, because he is not sure whether you enjoyed the story. He will look for approval from you, and in so doing, will automatically hold you in higher regard than a few moments ago. You, on the other hand, have heard the story, know some additional things about the speaker, *have a full claim to having had a conversation with the speaker*, yet have given away nothing. The end result is that, with respect to the speaker, you are one step "closer" and one step "higher" than you were before the conversation, yet no more familiar to him.

I heard a broadcast interview once with I forget whom on I forget what show where the speaker related an anecdote about how he once found himself sitting next to Quentin Tarantino. For thirty minutes straight, Tarantino talked about himself, the great work he was doing, and his movies, and then he got up and thanked the speaker for one of the best conversations he had ever had. This demonstrates ultimate conversation mastery (or, at least, the fact that people generally love to talk about themselves and like anyone who listens).

As a corporate employee, you may be told from time to time by mediocre managers to act friendlier, to let people get to know you, to reveal more of your brilliant personality. *Do not fall into this trap!* While, for the mediocre manager, this advice serves as a zero-effort way of giving some kind of feedback (since she cannot be bothered to look at your actual performance and results) and also gives her a short-cut in the future to evaluate you based on your personality and not your accomplishments, for you, this approach will lead to guaranteed loss of status. Like Eve's apple, this poisonous suggestion should be categorically rejected (*sotto voce*). Nod, seemingly agree with your manager, and then immediately banish the thought.

To reiterate the core concept of this chapter: remember to **stay aloof but interesting**. In this way, the mediocre employee gains all the benefits of corporate society without any of the potential negative side effects. Read on for some other specific situations where this rule must be remembered and followed.

A common occurrence in modern corporations is the out-of-office social affair. Most often, they take the shape of after-work drinks, holiday parties, and the occasional bring-your-family-to-the-park barbecue. Of course, all the communication methods outlined above apply in these situations as well, but another rule is even more important: **show up, leave early**. It is essential to register your presence at as many events as you can. In this way, you act the team player and do not permit the buildup of any amount of resentment from noted absences. However, just as important: do not stay long. First, there is no need: making sure everyone of importance sees you within the duration of, say, half an hour is sufficient to credit your attendance in their psychological memories of you; once you have achieved this goal, go do something really useful or interesting with your time. Second: by staying longer, you significantly risk descending into the relaxing comfort of familiarity, which, as you know by now, breeds contempt. At these social events, chitchat about work quickly dissipates, leaving you no choice but to become friendly and intimate with your co-workers. The mediocre employee knows to avoid this and will leave before this phase of the party commences. Let someone else continue on and accidentally tell unacceptable jokes, take flirtations too far into the realm of harassment, or get drunk and make a fool of himself dancing on the table. The mediocre employee is long-gone, enjoying his personal time with his real friends.

Having attended hundreds of such events, it has been my observation that the most successful employees typically show up for just an hour or so and then leave before the big drinking starts. In the case of managers, the more senior they are, the earlier they leave. For gala events, such as Christmas parties where attendance is particularly noted, the rule of thumb that I have observed is that the most senior manager typically will leave one-third of the way through the scheduled event. For example, if a party is planned from 7:00 p.m. to 4:00 a.m., the senior vice president is gone by 10:00 p.m.; by 1:00 a.m., no director (with any future in the company) will still be at the party.

The best way to leave when it is your time is to simply slip away. Do not worry about saying good-bye, as doing so will checkpoint and draw attention to your exit. Nobody will miss you, because everyone else is busy partying. If you do get pressed for an excuse, the best answer is "family commitments"; do not bother to explain further. The worst excuse is that you still have work to do; even if it is true, everyone will think you are lying or kissing up to management. Resist the temptation to use it.

One further word is warranted on the topic of getting drunk with co-workers: it is not worth it. Even if you like drinking and put value in a free wet bar, the harm to your reputation and the resulting negative perception of you by corporate decision makers is too great a price to pay. Unless you live in the 1960s or in certain parts of Eastern Europe (in which case you are not the target audience for this book), being able to "hold your liquor" is no longer a qualification for success. Consider that you have probably never seen your manager's manager drunk; if you aspire to that position one day, it is best not to let your subordinates see you drunk, either. An all-night booze-up might be great fun to discuss with your peers the next day, but it leaves only blemishes on your reputation with management (even if they left the party early, they will certainly get all the negative juicy details of your embarrassing behaviour from their water cooler discussions the next day).

Once I attended a corporate social event for a team of forty which was held overnight at an offsite camping location. With nowhere to go and nothing to do but drink alcohol, the evening's activities soon degenerated into the predictable *a cappella* karaoke and games of truth or dare. Even the ranking manager was forced to participate—there was nowhere to go! The subsequent embarrassment for all the drinkers was extreme; for the remainder of their careers at that company, they apologised to those who stayed sober for their various confessions of infidelity, perversions, and lascivious acts. (Fortunately for them, at least the group manager soon transitioned to another department, as predicted by Chapter 1).

A final word on avoiding familiarity at the workplace: it extends to the way you look. Although there is always the well-known exhortation to dress for the job you want, not the job you have, this book makes one simple easy-to-remember recommendation: do not wear blue jeans. Jeans are what you wear in your living room, to the pub with your mates, and so forth. Jeans give your colleagues one small subconscious excuse to not take you seriously. If you find yourself talking to someone in legwear that is baggy or overly tight and revealing or bleached out or roughly hewn, how does your subtle perception of that person change? If this psychological argument does not sway you, then consider the empirical one: how often do you see your manager's manager wearing jeans? Perhaps only at the annual company picnic (for the one hour that he is in attendance). He knows that jeans signal familiarity, and familiarity, as everyone knows, breeds contempt.

◇　◇　◇

It is now time for an exercise in mediocrity. Practice the concepts in this chapter. Choose the correct thing to say in each situation:

Situation 1: You and three colleagues are sitting at the lunch table in the break room, splitting apart your wooden chopsticks in preparation to dig into your takeout sushi. *You say:*

A) "So, Jane, how was your trip to the countryside this past weekend?"

B) "I'm planning my trekking holiday to Nepal for next year. It's going to be amazing. I've started buying my gear and planning the route. . . ."

C) "I'm so glad to be finally back in an office building. The six months I spent looking for this job was tough. I love it here."

Situation 2: You pass your manager in the hall and he is in a good mood. *You say:*

A) "This floor is like a D&D map! I'm trying to find conference room 2B, and it seems like I've been wondering the halls for hours!"

B) "Nice tie. Brad Pitt called; he wants to cast it in his next movie."

C) "I'll have that report to you by next week. It's going great."

Situation 3: You are at an office party, and it is getting towards 11pm. You are thinking it is time to head home. *You say:*

A) "Hey guys, it's been awesome. I'm taking off. See you on Monday."

B) Nothing.

C) "This party is crazy! I'm going to get drunk and dance all night long!"

Answers:

1:B—an interesting topic, divulging nothing personal related to work or performance (A gives away the opportunity to be interesting to someone else; C points out your weaknesses). **2:B**—it is funny, without being overly insulting (A makes you sound like a clueless geek; C is just not interesting). **3:B**—say nothing, just slip away (A brings needless attention to your departure; C will result in even more attention to your looking like an idiot the next day).[13]

---

13 Note that all the answers are B. The mediocre employee will also look for patterns in his work, which avoids having to think about the underlying reasoning. In this case, there is no particular correlation between answer B and the desired outcome, but still, it is a good habit to have. If there was a Situation 4, you should guess B, you might be right: you would have a 33 percent chance of it, while expending zero effort—an infinite ROI!

CHAPTER 5
Hello, Operator!

Just as in the olden days, when switchboard operators were responsible for making the connections that carried messages from one party to another, so must you manage the communication flow around your corporation; it does not manage itself. Although good employees go about doing the company's business, the mediocre employee will invest a significant proportion of his time in playing the "operator" if he wishes to succeed. He will make the connections if and when he chooses, between the parties he needs, and even partially control the messages being transmitted. Get in the habit of imagining yourself coming in to the switchboard desk every day as you commute to your office.

The primary guiding principle to keep in mind is that a lot less communication takes place inside your corporation than a reasonable person would expect. Such reasonableness would dictate that problems, negatives, issues to solve, performance details, achievements, and so forth be discussed, evaluated, jointly solved, and communicated to the right people at the right time. But, because results are hardly ever measured, no one really likes to go around talking about them. There is instead a general preference towards *abstract qualitative positivity*—that is, maintaining a vague sense that things are generally okay without going into details. On occasion, someone may admit things are not going so well but laughs it off anyway. [14] Thus, most important information never flows to where it needs to go.

The higher up the management hierarchy, the less communication actually occurs. This is partially due to executives' having less time to devote to the different issues with which they are dealing, but mostly this rarefied communication is primarily due to executives' being far more sparing with their communication than the lower level plebes. When they talk to each other, or when plebes talk to them, they are even more reluctant to mention problems or to volunteer information. Discussing problems would increase the risk of being seen as incompetent by their peers, and volunteering information would subject them to additional questioning and potential responsibilities. So the abstract qualitative positivity becomes even more pronounced at more senior levels. Formal communication sessions are very tightly time-boxed and compartmentalised, as is face time with direct reports. This means that, when communicating with them, negative things must be carefully condensed, requests must be triaged, and positive things must compete for time with the first two. Executives

---

14   The Alec Baldwin speech from the movie *Glengarry Glen Ross* (based on the play by David Mamet) is an exception that proves the rule. As the guys are sitting in the office gossiping on a rainy evening, Blake gathers them and says: "Let me have your attention for a moment! So you're talking about what? You're talking about . . . bitching about that sale you shot, some son of a bitch that doesn't want to buy, somebody that doesn't want what you're selling, some broad you're trying to screw and so forth. *Let's talk about something important.*" What makes this scene so famously powerful is that you have probably never heard that kind of focus on results from a senior boss before. In corporations, they are often as complicit in abstract qualitative positivity as everyone else.

will claim that this is because they are short on time, but the truth is that this is the way they prefer to limit their personal liability.

When I was working in a large global corporation, at one point, an annual promotion committee meeting was held in the afternoon of a Western time zone, despite the fact that the plurality of the rest of the company was located in the East, eight time zones away. The VP of my department decided not to call in to the late-night meeting, even though he was the designated representative and advocate of his fifty-eight-person team at this meeting (he did send a junior director who happened to be in the West as his proxy). This made it very convenient for both the promotion committee and the VP to avoid responsibility for the resultantly low rate of promotion for his team. The promotion committee members would say that their executives were all so busy that the meeting could not take place at any other time in the day (even though, ostensibly, evaluating promotions should have been the most important part of their job). The VP would say that the committee made it impossible for him to attend, given the scheduled time of the meeting (though advocating for his team should have been the most important part of his job). The truth was that the company was trying to limit promotions through the tactic of indirectly limiting communication, whereas our department had done a lot of great work and accumulated much seniority and expected just reward. To reduce the corporate excuse to its essence: there was not enough time to properly execute the promotion review! Within a year, 30 percent of the department had left the company, and 60 percent was gone within two years. But by that point, the VP had long since transferred back to the Western headquarters and was put in charge of a new department. Remember—results don't matter, including and especially employee retention results. The promotion committee members all remained in their jobs, of course, for a long time (Chapter 7 may help explain why).

But fear not, mediocre employee! You can use all of this to your advantage within your corporation *by counting on bad information being lost or by injecting additional good information at strategic points.* As already mentioned, the mechanics for doing this involve the same mechanics a nosy switchboard operator would employ—strategically connecting two parties either by making a connection that would not otherwise exist, preventing a connection, or routing it through a third party to transform the message. As part of either approach, the timing of the connection often plays part. And, finally, the words of the message itself can be altered or shaped by the operator (think of the traditionally amusing cinematographic analogy: "shhhh *the line* shhhhh *is static-y* shhhhh *can't hear, too much noise* shhhh . . ." when one party purposely fakes a bad mobile phone signal to escape having to acknowledge the message of the other party). But the actual mechanics are the easy part once you examine your particular organisation to see how to play operator. As you assume this role, the *content* of the communication will be the more critical part. Some highly effective genres of such information manipulation are outlined in the rest of this chapter.

A flagship method that is effective for the mediocre employee almost without fail is: **always claim success**. This is not only an issue of the words you use, but your body language, your enthusiasm, and even your state of mind. *Project success.* Your initiatives are *always* going well; spin them that way. At every opportunity, highlight the positives. Reinforce the perception that you are doing great work. If someone, including your manager, asks you how a project is going, the generically correct answer is always: *"It's going* *great. We* [or "I", if you can get away with it] *have accomplished X and Y. Z is causing us some problems, but we're already executing a plan to overcome it.* " Your manager might, on occasion, actually know what is going on, in which case you can add, *"A isn't done yet but I'm all over it, and B failed, but this just helped us learn how to deal with C, which is now going great"* and so on and so forth. People *want* to hear that things are well. Make them feel *good*—tell them what they want to hear! Moreover, you will be perceived to be an effective employee and good at your job. It is just basic human psychology.

In the case where it is manifestly evident that a project is not going well (and this might be a nonnegligible risk for a mediocre employee), do not fear, for the approach to this is the same—*treat it as a win, anyway!* Never mention the loss. Dress it up like a win, feed it like a win, and put it to bed like a win. Instead of saying to your colleague, *"my manager chewed me out because I was late and the numbers didn't add up right"*, you should say, *"he gave me some great advice on how to make it even better and encouraged me to spend more time on it"*. If it looks like a win, waddles like a win, and quacks like a win, it *must* be a win, right? Very few people in your organisation have the time or energy to bother to figure out that it is actually a duck. Almost everyone will think you are a regular winner.

So what is the downside of this approach? Logic would dictate that if a project is indeed *not* going well or, even worse, fails in the end, you would look more foolish or even incompetent claiming that it was a success all along than you would if you had made more objective and honest evaluations of it earlier on. In the corporate environment, this is a very wrong analysis that conscientious employees often try to utilise. By doing this, they are ignoring several lessons already discussed in this book: (a) almost no one ever measures results, so it will be hard for anyone to contradict you with factual information and say that the project actually did not go well. Moreover, your peers or other peripheral managers will actually never know at all, because they are usually worried about their own projects, not yours; (b) it is generally unlikely you will even be around to face the people to whom you made representations about how the project was going by the time enough information exists to question you about it; and (c) even if evidence emerges, *and* the same parties are still around, so much time will have elapsed that almost no one will remember what you said or care to bring up ancient conversations from many months or years ago. And if in the extremely rare case that this perfect storm does occur and someone makes the effort to challenge you along the lines of, *"Hey, you told me twelve months ago that the project was going well, and now that we've had six months of data, it's performing very poorly"*, your simple response is, *"It* was *going well twelve months ago but a few things fell through at the last minute"*. So, you see, unyieldingly positive self-evaluations offer no significant downside to the mediocre employee.

Hand in hand with your qualitatively positive claims about your successes should go your views about your own skills and your efforts—**never disparage yourself or your own work**. There is simply no need to do so. Just as the previous chapter on performance evaluation has discussed, false modesty, even in jest, will not serve the mediocre employee well. As the English author Antony Trollope said, "Nobody holds a good opinion of man who has a low opinion of himself". Why bring attention to something that you may, in fact, not be good at, or to a project that may, in fact, not be that important? *Everything you work on is extremely important to the company business; position it as such.* You are *not* compiling a monthly report on the expense figures for the stationery cupboard; you are *"facilitating cost savings across the* *organisation towards meeting the profitability targets of Q1*". You are *not* doing yet another presentation on market share that a monkey could do in its sleep and that you have done (in your sleep) dozens of times before; you are *"informing senior management's critical decision points related to the brand growth dynamic and the changing competitive environment"*. Never ever bring attention to your mediocrity! Usually, no one else will, because it would be considered rude and unprofessional to challenge you publicly, and most people will have neither the time nor the personal capital to go behind your back to rectify your exaggerations to management.

If you do feel the need to joke or to otherwise admit weaknesses (some companies' unofficial social cultures do indeed subtly encourage this type of self-denigration to facilitate bonding, and any nonparticipants are considered arrogant or aloof), you should limit yourself to disparaging anything *not* related to work. It is moderately acceptable to not be good at golf or playing the violin or to have unruly children (unless you work in Sales, in which case never admit your golfing failures!). But the mediocre employee should never disparage a self trait that might ever be referenced in the workplace. Likewise, she should never use such phrases as, *"Yeah, that task was no big deal; I was able to do it pretty quickly over the weekend and get it out of the way"*. That approach acts as a minimiser of the importance and difficulty of the project and the importance it has to the company. Instead, always seek to **maximise** it: *"I felt it was important to spend some weekend time to make sure this task could serve effectively as the building block of the larger project due next month"*. The task did not change, the effort on your part did not change—but the difference in phrasing that will improve the perception your colleagues have of you versus the one that would actually hurt it should be obvious not just to the mediocre employee. Remember from the previous chapter: the more people perceive that you are working on projects that are important, even critical, to company business, the more they will generally think that you are important to the company and to management and that you are an effective and capable employee.

Once you get the hang of never disparaging your own work but instead trying to maximise its perceived importance at every opportunity, you should start to look for what are commonly called **Quick Wins**. In many companies, this is actually a fully encouraged and industrialised process by which groups or individuals look for short, easy tasks or projects that can be completed and presented to management with some claim to success or accomplishment. Quick Wins usually are the first few obvious steps of a long project, the "low-hanging fruit" that bear value immediately, or the tasks with the highest visibility. The entire and only point of the exercise is to give management, the project sponsor, or other colleagues *the impression* that the team or individual is capable of delivering quickly, continuously, and ostensibly with results. Manipulation of perception is built into this approach *by definition*—and that is precisely why it is so effective and is recommended to the mediocre employee. This approach is very fruitful in corporations because:

a) A few quick wins often successfully relax management's oversight over the project or employee, because management perceives rapid topical progress and accomplishment (usually without bothering to look under the hood) and gives flexibility to future work.

b) Quick wins permit the employee to defer the difficult parts of the project to a later point, where the likelihood of management, the employee, or project priorities shifting around entirely are much higher and possibly will allow avoidance of the difficult parts altogether.

c) Quick wins permit racking up mentionable accomplishments in case project priorities do change and the employee is reassigned or in case the quarterly performance review is right around the corner and needs some juicing.

Always look for Quick Wins, and you will almost always come out ahead. It is certainly not the same approach as working on the tasks with the highest ROI to your company, the highest likelihood of long-term success, the biggest financial impact, or on tasks that actually materially impact results. But as a way of creating and delivering messages that you want your managers to hear, few tools are better than Quick Wins to a skilled operator from the mediocre class.

In one corporation where I spent several years, many mid-level managers utilised this approach almost exclusively. They would start every big project with a public and explicit discussion of the Quick Wins the team should pursue and how to position them to senior management. Indeed, my own manager often suggested I look for quick wins that I could present to executives to boost my perceived performance. Because this company did a localised organisational restructuring every year and a global reorganisation every two years, and because the average employee tenure there was about three years, and if work got too difficult it was not so hard to transfer to another department, an employee could spend his entire career there pursuing only quick-win projects and do well. A number of mediocre employees at this company did exactly that. Unfortunately, this did little to help the company's stock price, which has not increased in eleven years (adjusting for inflation).

This chapter earlier discussed how organisations often lose information as it flows along communication channels. For the advanced operator, the time dimension of this phenomenon can also be of great utility. *Institutional memory* is the concept of what a company knows over time, and, as with human memory, most things eventually fade from the collective consciousness of a corporation. As people leave, as priorities change, or as individuals simply forget, institutional memory retains but a tiny percentage of the knowledge that got broadcast across the transom (which is itself a small percentage of all the information that existed in the company). Even in companies that try to set up knowledge bases or other formal mechanisms for retaining information, 95 percent of all recognised knowledge will probably be gone within a three-year cycle, and another 4 percent within the following two years. Attempts to document knowledge usually end in thick files on dusty shelves that no one will ever look at until trash collectors come to bin them when the company goes under (e.g., performance reviews, quarterly results, congratulations for achievements). Or it is found in individuals' e-mail archives that are quickly forgotten as employees try to process their ever-growing inboxes until they eventually leave their roles and the IT department purges the accounts. The little bit of knowledge that can be retained is restricted to highly specialised data that is kept in strictly formatted, easy-to-search repositories that barely make sense to someone looking at it several years later (e.g., market-share statistics, technical specifications, production levels). This type of formal information is almost always quality-agnostic and will rarely be traced to you anyway; so, overall, you are generally safe to assume that knowledge bases and repositories do *not* work and are of no consequence to you in the organisation.

The other locus of institutional memory, and one that you *should* care about, lies in the minds of people who have worked with you before. As already discussed in this book, their perception of you is acquired in various ways and impacts the evaluation and feedback they recycle back into the system (to your manager, to the promotion committee, and so forth). Although it is hard to impose change on these perceptions once they are formulated, just like any memories, they fade over time, get replaced by more important things, or simply decrease in importance to their holders. Any reminders or reference points they may have had to reinforce their perceptions also disappear over time: quarterly reports get filed away, growth charts shift the relevant time window ever forward, metrics get absorbed and diluted in the larger context of the corporation. Moreover, as these people leave the company or your department or get promoted, you can safely assume that their replacements will have no significant knowledge about your projects or previous performance besides perhaps what can be transmitted within a three-minute chat with the departed. Most things will simply not get passed along. As far as the mediocre employee should be concerned, institutional memory lasts only about as long as you are in the reporting hierarchy of your manager's manager.

So, what does this mean to you, that mediocre employee? It means you can **utilise the lack of institutional memory to your advantage**. Firstly, do not worry if a project fails or underperforms—most people will forget, and evidence will disappear quickly. The two or three people of importance who do not forget and stick around, perhaps including your manager and some of her peer managers, will indeed need additional "work" from you to overcome their residual perception. And here is where mediocrity itself is such a boon. The mediocre employee need not be overly concerned with truth or accuracy—his mediocrity more freely permits him this leeway. He can simply begin to omit negative points or issues from discussion while refreshing the beneficial points. For example, he does *not* need to remind people with whom he talks that the Q2 marketing campaign failed to produce any boost in sales; he can instead remind them how effectively he designed the collateral and worked with the media partner to coordinate the launch. He can even go so far as to reinvent things in a completely different light after some time has passed (remember to always trend towards claiming success, as discussed earlier in this book). The big launch of the new product in Q1 of last year did *not* fizzle, resulting in a complete abort and pulling of the product from distribution; instead, the launch prepared the marketplace for the subsequently better products that were launched this year while keeping competition out of the news. It was planned this way from the very beginning! As operator, use the weakness of institutional memory to your advantage in combination with the well-known psychological phenomenon that *if you repeat something often enough, (most) people will start to believe it.*[15]

Another aspect of corporate communication that novice employees often ignore is the very slow velocity of personal praise. **Do not wait for your manager to praise you**, and, most certainly, do not assume he praises you to other people. Likely to be a mediocre employee himself, his typical inclination will be to take credit for your work (*remember, he plays operator on his own behalf, too!*), and he will almost always only assign credit to you when it costs him nothing or does not detract from his own glory. Moreover, as already discussed, he probably has a limited amount of

---

15   The approach and its variations were extensively studied and formulated by none other than Adolf Hitler and his Minister of Propaganda, Joseph Goebbels, in a concept Hitler dubbed "the Big Lie" ("Joseph Goebbels," *Wikipedia*, http://en.wikiquote.org/wiki/Joseph_Goebbels#Misattributed (2011).).

time to talk about things like how great members of his team are when meeting with his manager or with other groups. Thus, it is a grave mistake to focus on doing work and expecting everyone to somehow know how great you are for doing it. No one will know unless you tell them. So, as your own operator, make sure you spend a fair amount of your vocal power on singing your own praises, be it to your manager or to other senior managers, but, most especially, to your manager's manager. You need to get around the praise-absorber that is your manager and *make sure* his manager hears the positives you want him to know. Force that direct connection: drop by for quick questions, corner him by the water cooler, and actively seek him out to explain your accomplishments. Even if your manager's manager is reluctant to engage (so he can pass the buck for any potential responsibility back down to your direct manager), force the issue, and push it without shame. It always pays dividends.[16]

Beware also of the following situation: often, your manager might say *"I'm working hard for you"*, or *"I talked to the big boss to get you that promotion"*. But do not believe him; he could be outright lying (he is an operator, too!), and you have no way of knowing. In my career, I have encountered a significant number of managers who made similar claims. It is a very effective, insidious, and possibly misleading way to build up goodwill, patience, and loyalty, because there is really no way to disprove your manager's promise, and it is plausibly explainable if nothing comes of it: *"I tried for*

---

16   As a side note: the same logic applies *to problems or complaints* you have about colleagues. Do not use the performance review process as a mechanism for delivering this feedback; formal upward feedback does not really register or matter (Chapter 3). Hand-deliver your feedback to the most relevant manager (in conversation, e-mail, and so forth). This book does not advocate making up damaging claims against colleagues, but do remember that unless you deliver the message directly to the appropriate destination, the problems will usually never surface to see the light of day.

you, but the big boss just has too many other priorities, and the salary raise pot is fixed and the number of promotions capped. Sorry, I'll try again for you next year." On many occasions, I have dug further, asked colleagues, and even talked to the big boss and found out that my mediocre manager had never even come close to doing the things he promised on my behalf.

Take the approach of singing your own praises up even farther up the chain of command, and **cultivate the promotion committee** as much as you can. Find out who the people are who actually make promotion and raise decisions and try to make sure you are on their radar, again, without assuming your manager will put you there. Although your manager might be your formal advocate for about five minutes once a year when your promotion review comes up, an intervention that small almost assures you will not profit from it. In organisations that consider themselves progressive, the promotion committee might be a big group, which is all the more reason to get yourself known by as many of them as possible. Consider the math: in a promotion committee of ten members, a lightly positive endorsement of you from five members is significantly more powerful than a strong endorsement of you from one member. Even promotion committee members who are not directly in your chain of command or your job function can be engaged and messaged. For personal reputation, in corporations, *breadth is much more valuable than depth* (and depth can actually turn dangerous, because depth draws scrutiny, scrutiny yields familiarity, and, as you remember, familiarity breeds contempt!). The mediocre employee must never forget to frequently turn her head to the sky and yell on her own behalf as loudly as possible so fabulous tales of her goodness travel to the most remote VPs in the land.

Finally, the most advanced form of playing operator is actually becoming a *full-time* operator for an executive or group. **Command HQ Operator is actually a very good strategic role in a corporation.** If you can become good at passing messages between important people, you will become trusted and valued, which is good, and you will be required to do less actual work, which is even better. If possible to position herself in such a role, a mediocre employee will try her hand at doing summary reports, overview presentations, quarterly newsletters, and so forth. If you are at Command HQ, you are safe in the bunker with the generals, eating at their canteen, not at the Front, rotting in a trench. A mediocre employee will actively seek out such a role, thereby positioning herself for potentially significant success.[17]

At one large corporation where I worked, a low-level newly graduated associate got the coveted job of being the assistant to the group's senior VP. After a year of playing operator (coordinating meetings, writing summary notes, issuing reports) side-by-side with the SVP, it was time for him to rotate out, and, of course, he was given his choice of assignments anywhere in the world. Naturally, he chose the most fruitful one, in another geographic region. By virtue of working on this juicy assignment and his connections back at HQ, his success in the company was assured, and he was quickly promoted above all the local group members who had spent years actually *doing* the group's work. At another large corporation where I worked, a particularly talentless and mediocre manager stepped on the escalator right at the point where the company was beginning global expansion.

---

17   In German companies, this has actually been formalised into a role known as "executive assistant," which is extremely coveted and pursued by elite graduates of the best schools. It is considered a very senior role, not to be confused with the same title in U.S. companies, where it is a junior administrative role (i.e., "secretary"). Executive assistants in large German corporations work alongside C-level or even board members and write their own tickets from then on.

But as the first manager in this area, she became the *de facto* coordinator and distributor of information and organiser of global summits, reports, and, eventually, resources. This role, and her access to the executives, eventually put her in position where she had more control of the information flow on the global situation than anyone else, and thus she became VP of International. Unfortunately, she had little talent for things like decision making, managing employees, strategic analysis, and so forth, so she had to limit herself to chairing meetings and making speeches. Alas, this was very little help to everyone else in the international departments who were trying to do the company's business. She was replaced after a few years, but she is now happily retired as a former VP of a large global corporation.

$$\text{🖒} \quad \text{🖒} \quad \text{🖒}$$

Now it is your turn: connect the message on the left with the destination on the right to which you would actively direct it. Being an operator requires lots of practice and even thought!

Message	Destination
✉ A) Your manager says: *"You did a really great job on this project. Thanks."*	
✉ B) Your manager says: *"This project is a complete failure. You need to figure out how to fix it ASAP; ask others for help."*	🖅 Your boss
✉ C) Some other manager says: *"I'm not sure you should be assigned to this project. Check with your boss."*	🖅 Your boss's boss
✉ D) Your manager says: *"I'm going to assign you to this special project. It's a great opportunity."*	🖅 Other managers
✉ E) A peer says: *"I'm sick of this project we're working on. I don't want to work on it, I'm sure you'll finish it on your own."*	🖅 Other peers
✉ F) You've just seen that the Sales numbers have gone up this year, even though you transferred out of the Sales department last year.	🏛 NO ONE!

If you want to check your answers to the above exercise to see if you got the correct results, do not worry about it. Results don't matter.

Instead, continue on quickly to the next project: write some of your own messages that you can "introduce" into the transom of your own volition. Example message: *"I just had an excellent meeting with Manager Jim. He really likes the approach we are taking on this project and liked my presentation."* ⇨ **delivered to your boss.**

Your Message 1: _____ ⇨
delivered to your boss

Your Message 2: _____ ⇨
delivered to your boss's boss

Your Message 3: _____ ⇨
delivered to your group VP who is on the promotion committee

Of course, you can effectively play operator in many other ways. This chapter presents a few key ones. Use your imagination to develop your own techniques based on the specifics of your corporation. Connect your own endpoints based on the characteristics of your co-workers. Just remember, *communication is most often what informs perceptions.* And as the mediocre reader knows already from this book, perceptions are what really matter.

CHAPTER 6
Wherefore HR?

Without spending too much time on this topic, it is important to devote a special chapter to, just as Hell reserves a special level for, the corporate Human Resources department. This book touches upon many aspects of organisational behaviour, corporate structure, personal interaction, and relations between colleagues. In essence, it primarily deals with the actual "human resources" of a corporation (which includes you, the mediocre employee!) and how it is possible to extract the most personal benefit and utility from them using various effective methods. But by no means should you confuse actual "human resources" with the Human Resources *department* in your corporation, whose goal and entire essence of being is largely *unrelated* to these objectives. As it turns out, in corporations, the HR department serves very little positive purpose, despite its apparently outsize importance. Moreover, its structure and traditionally defined position more often damages the company, instead. Mediocre employees must avoid HR at all costs, except for limited exploitative purposes.

First, it is important to recognise why corporate HR departments continue to exist despite generally universal employee disapprobation: they fulfil their roles of keeping administrative paperwork, following legal requirements to avoid lawsuits, and processing paychecks and benefits. And that is where their positive contributions end. Beyond this, HR serves only the purpose of its masters—the senior executives. Almost as a rule, HR has no accountability, an abstract budget rooted in nothing specific (and that must be spent in any case), and results that are by nature impossible to measure on anything but a very long-term basis.[18]

The key to understanding how HR gets into this position is to realise that, over time, as a small company becomes a corporation, HR takes on the role of a "shield" to which executives can delegate unpleasant tasks and redirect the ire or complaints of employees. HR then feels empowered to insert itself into things like hiring, evaluating performance, influencing promotion decisions, and influencing the character and even strategy of the company.

Moreover, as the HR department becomes the cornerstone of a corporate bureaucracy (towards which it is inevitably pushed by the ever-increasing emphasis on following rules and checking boxes), HR managers have to continue to make themselves seem necessary and busy. At this point, HR begins to "invent" new things to do, such as inserting itself into the performance review process or even trying to reengineer it entirely. This overhaul invariably makes it

---

18   A company "will never catch the real cost of its HR department's action. Human resources can readily provide the number of people it hired, the percentage of performance evaluations completed, and the extent to which employees are satisfied or not with their benefits. But only rarely does it link any of those metrics to business performance." This quote is from a good article: Keith H. Hammonds, "Why We Hate HR," *Fast Company*, http://www.fastcompany.com/magazine/97/open_hr.html (2005). The reader is advised to read the article for a deeper explanation of the problems with HR than this chapter provides.

more complicated and less useful but permits HR managers to point out improvements they are making (using the erroneous but easily swallowed logic that "complexity = improvement"). Alternatively, HR will endeavour to roll out new abstract concepts, such as "corporate behaviours/ beliefs", and then invent new ways to spend employees' time on training or indoctrination in the same. As it happens, these are some of the same behaviours recommended to mediocre employees in other chapters in this book, so HR can often serve as a model to mediocre employees throughout the rest of the company.

A wonderful example of this comes from a company where I worked that had gone through a period of large growth and rapid hiring. That came to an end as the business matured and the economy took a pause, so the HR department started to get bored. The company had a six-point short-and-sweet "mission statement" that initially guided the philosophy of the company from its early days. HR renamed these "behaviours", added five to eight sub-bullets to each one, and then rolled them out to the entire corporation as a cultural refinement. Then, all employees were obligated to go through a two-day training course during which these fifty or so total sub-behaviours were explained in painful detail and employees drew pictures, role played, and completed various other learning activities in the hopes of absorbing them. And to top off the fun, HR then mandated that these behaviours be used as the categories and framework for doing self- and peer evaluations during all future performance review cycles. The fact that none of the "behaviours" in the framework actually focused on results or benefit to the company was surely just a small oversight on the part of HR.

Surely, the litany of problems with HR is ample enough for academic chairs to be endowed just to research the topic, but more important to you is what the mediocre employee should do regarding HR. The answer: **avoid, avoid, avoid dealing with HR**, except tactically. Simply: do not complain to HR; do not ask HR for assistance; do not look to HR for corporate justice or to right a wrong. Do not try to build a relationship with HR, unless it is one of telling the department what to do (by which time, you are probably an executive already, so congratulations!). Learn to function without the HR department, and when someone tells you that HR approval is needed for something, ignore this and get the approval from the actual manager most relevantly interested in its happening. As a regular mediocre employee, you are unlikely to be in a position to positively direct the actions of HR, but you will instead probably unduly draw its attention and ire for disturbing the peace.

Just as importantly, **do not socialise with HR managers**, because they will be taking mental notes about your managerial ability and fit within the corporate culture they imagine they are building. Familiarity breeds contempt, and, even if you overcome this through sheer charm, having a positive perception from an HR manager will not get you promoted (whereas a negative perception can very easily derail your success). Imagine the promotion committee: ten managers and an HR manager sitting around a table. Five senior managers chime in about how good you are, and the HR manager adds his voice, by which point it is pretty irrelevant (he is just an HR manager, so who cares?). On the other hand, picture the same scenario with a slight twist: of the ten managers sitting around a table, five offer their support to promoting you, but the HR manager has taken a disliking to you and begins a long diatribe about how you are unsuited for the role, not mature enough, have had personal interaction problems, and so forth. It becomes much harder to argue with such qualitative evaluations, and the argument might sway the promotion committee against you. Thus, socialising with HR managers offers no net benefit. Socialising moderately with HR *staff*, however, is acceptable: you might need them to sign some paperwork one day or tell you what your manager's salary is.

Ostensibly, Human Resources (it is useful to occasionally recall the original meaning of the phrase) positions itself as a mediator of problems between employees, as well. HR may even promise confidentiality and advocacy on your behalf. The mediocre employee will remember that **under no circumstances should she take real, personal problems to HR to resolve**. This includes problems or disagreements with performance reviews, job-function disputes with managers, inappropriate project assignments, and so forth. Remember, it is not in the interest of HR to take your side; by default, HR takes the side of the more senior person. HR managers are neither rewarded nor compensated for "justice". Instead, they are rewarded for keeping a tight ship with no flare-ups of conflict and are more likely to quickly throw you overboard than to let you foment mutiny. If you try to appeal to HR for something that requires an HR manager to choose your interests over those of some other employee, this will end your progression at that company rather quickly.

If you are an audacious mediocre employee, you may actually attempt to co-opt HR in another way. Consider that HR is more than happy to jump into action only in the circumstance *when no preference between employees needs to be expressed*. This occurs in situations where an employee is perceived to have "violated" some rule, the code of conduct, the law, and so forth, and the conflict is one against "the rules" rather than in relation to another employee. In doing so, HR can appear relevant, heroic, even, by enforcing the strict moral codes of the company without stepping on the toes of any employees who should remain at the company once the dust has settled. In corporations, it is easier to get fired for lying on your résumé, sexual harassment, or cheating on your expenses than for gross incompetence in performing your job.[19] If the mediocre employee sees something of this transgressive nature being carried out by a rival, an unpleasant co-worker, or an otherwise-disliked peer (never a senior manager, though!), she can **choose to bring these transgressions to the attention of HR**. Some may call this backstabbing, but the mediocre employee knows that it is simply helping ensure that the right rules are being followed at the company. Be careful of this tactic, because, although it does not directly assign you demerit, it puts you on the radar of HR in a negatively related context; from that point on, you will have to carefully manage your HR profile.

At one of my former corporate employers, one colleague once let slip a single, somewhat-sexist remark in the presence of his female manager. I was present and thus know the exact matter. HR swung into full, delighted action, and, over the next several weeks, interviewed witnesses (including me), took written depositions, consulted the dusty rule books, formulated official position statements, and, in the end, convinced the long-serving and knowledgeable employee that his career at the company was over. He announced his own departure several weeks later, and HR was very happy with itself for having done such a diligent job in ensuring that the best interests of the company were served.

---

19   Firing someone for incompetence in a corporation (say, losing the company a million dollars) requires clear evidence of assignable inadequacy (already, an almost impossible task, because results are rarely tracked), several cycles of documented poor performance reviews, possibly disciplinary hearings, paying out severance, possible exposure to litigation, and so forth. It is a lot of work and headache for HR. Firing someone for cheating on his expenses (say, a false claim for a hundred dollars) requires nothing more than some basic evidence and a director's sign-off.

In general, though, it is best to **avoid engaging HR for anything requiring actual company work.** A regular mediocre employee might think that inviting HR into a project will offload some of his own responsibilities or perhaps leverage some knowledge or skills that HR staff has. But, the mediocre employee who has read this book knows that this is a false illusion and that HR will instead slow the project down, weight it down with bureaucracy, and generally derail it from the optimal trajectory. Experienced managers know that if you want to slow down the recruiting and hiring process, give it to HR. If you want to minimise the value of training to your employees, let HR select and administer the training program. If you want to ensure that HR benefits are barely adequate, let HR choose and negotiate them with providers. If you want to bog down the performance review process in formal documentation, long delays, and useless writing, let HR reengineer it. Of course, in many cases, this outcome is *exactly* what mediocre managers want. So, perhaps it is best to reword the instruction from above: avoid engaging HR for anything requiring actual company work that you want to be executed smoothly and effectively.

Finally, earlier in this chapter, the mediocre employee is advised not to socialise with HR managers. Although socialising is proscribed, it is however moderately recommended to **turn up your personal propaganda** whenever they are around. The mediocre employee should look busy, talk a lot, spout ideas, be funny, and so forth (all the things described in Chapter 2) *even more emphatically* whenever HR managers are present. HR managers are even less capable of evaluating the true value of all the things you say or claim to have done than your peers or managers and are thus even more susceptible to personal propaganda. Also, feed the egos of HR managers—make them feel like they are important, write them memos, and even invite them to occasional meetings. Get them in your corner. Keep it strictly symbolic, though: do not actually ask them to *do* anything, to decide anything, or to take responsibility for anything, as you have already been forewarned of the consequences.[20] Your goal as a mediocre employee is to be noted by HR as a mover and shaker. Although the direct boost to your success at the next promotion committee meeting may be small, at least it helps convince HR to stay out of your way, which is itself very useful down the line when you need the flexibility. Even the Devil probably keeps the HR department on its very own level in Hell, because otherwise it just gets in the way.

👍   👍   👍

---

20   If you are wondering how HR gets involved in so many corporate activities in the first place, it is exactly this same process going on at management levels above you: senior managers inadvertently, or on purpose, get HR overly involved in various initiatives to build up their own personal propaganda or to consciously suboptimise things.

Question: Wherefore HR?

Answer: **Optimally, for nothing except self-promotion.**

Print or cut this out, laminate it, and carry it in your wallet, along with the "Corporate Values" card that HR already gave you:

My Values for My Company's HR

- Do not complain to HR.

- Do not socialise with HR managers.

- Do not depend on HR to solve problems.

- Use HR tactically against rivals.

- Do not try to get HR involved in any processes I manage, including hiring, if I want them done well.

- Turn up my personal propaganda when HR managers are around.

CHAPTER 7
Organisational Devolution

Devolution – descent or degeneration to a lower or worse state

Maybe your company was once great. Chances are, it is no longer so. *Most* companies are not, so do not be surprised. As a matter of fact, it is more likely than not that your corporation is going through even further devolution right now! Just a handful of companies either start out great in their first few years or exhibit occasional relatively brief spurts of greatness.[21] Most of the rest of the time, *all* companies are in a slow decline, both formerly great ones and never-great ones, until they reach some steady state of mediocrity. Note that this does *not* necessarily mean that their business is in decline or that their revenue is shrinking. It is quite possible that they may have found a fruitful business model to exploit, have established practices that continue to accelerate and to bear fruit via inertia, or have successfully cornered a market, thus

---

21   A well-regarded project led by a renowned researcher found only 11 companies that *improved* from good to great out of the *entire pool* of 1,435 Fortune 500 corporations between 1965 and 1995; Jim Collins, *Good to Great* (London: Random House, 2001), p. 220.

giving the company a continued appearance of "financial" success for some longer duration of time. But almost without exception, the internal operations, qualities, and abilities of the corporate body and its human resources are years further along in decline than its business performance.[22] One way to consider it is that business performance is a "trailing indicator" of the capability of a company. The corporate devolution to mediocrity begins long before the numbers start to show it.

Treatises exist on organisational behaviour and how to explain and to navigate it. However, such literature generally looks at the "steady-state" environment of corporations, where little changes over time, or it examines how to facilitate and to profit from "greatness seeking"—trying to make you or your company great. This chapter instead focuses on the situation that most corporations find themselves in most of the time—a generally steady state of devolution. Of course, this is particularly true at *recently* great companies, because the rate of decline is noticeably steeper; but it also applies to many other corporations at which you, the ambitious mediocre reader, may find yourself. Because you are mediocre, you are unlikely to get into the rare greatness-growth company (i.e., the top 5 percent). But because you are also ambitious, you are unlikely to choose a submediocre company (the bottom 50 percent). So, it is quite probable that you will be somewhere in the top fifth to fiftieth percentile

---

22   Scott Adams (of *Dilbert* comic strip fame) observes accurately: "When companies make money, we assume they are well-managed. That perception is reinforced by the CEOs of those companies who are happy to tell you all the clever things they did to make it happen. The problem with relying on this source of information is that CEOs are highly skilled in a special form of lying called leadership. Leadership involves convincing employees and investors that the CEO has something called a vision, a type of optimistic hallucination that can come true only in an environment in which the CEO is massively overcompensated and the employees have learned to be less selfish"; Scott Adams, "Betting on the Bad Guys," *The Wall Street Journal,* http://online.wsj.com/article/SB10001424052748704025304575285000265955016.html (2010).

of companies—*precisely* the ones devolving most acutely. The mediocre reader does not require extensive explanations of how to avoid or to reverse organisational devolution. Rather, this chapter provides the key tips on how to exploit it. Where it is helpful for understanding the required actions, the reasons why these conditions arise are also explained.

It has been accurately observed that "A students" hire A students because they want others of similar qualities working alongside them. Whereas: B students hire C students, because they do not want potential rivals or threats within the organisation. (And if a C student finds herself in a hiring position, any subsequent hires are as likely to be basically random as anything else, because C students are not terribly bothered by long-term planning.) The result of this heuristic is that, after some period of time, a company will eventually dilute itself to a whole lot of B and C employees. The inductive logic is simple: even if it starts out as all As, one inadvertent B who somehow slips past the hiring committee into the organisation will eventually spawn a whole host of subsequent Cs, and, from there, pure alphabetic chaos. Incidentally, this is one of the main, almost unavoidable, reasons that excellent corporations devolve (especially if HR gets involved in the hiring process, as previously explained). *Excellence is an unstable equilibrium.*

The mediocre employee will be very aware of this ongoing dynamic and will constantly keep an eye out for the opportunities it presents. In essence, this dynamic constitutes a type of instability, or volatility, in the hiring (or other talent acquisition) marketplace. And, just as the most successful financial traders make their profits off volatility, not investment, the mediocre employee will look for these openings and pounce. In your behaviour, this **means moving around a lot from company to company and from team to team**. Job loyalty lost its value somewhere in the 1990s, and it is more than acceptable these days to have a new job every two to three years on your résumé. Look for companies that are successful but are perhaps slightly past their maturity points and have opened up the doors to hiring from the general marketplace, because their early leaders and visionaries have begun to cash out (or "check out") and have reduced their oversight of the companies.[23] Or, if you are exploring within your current corporation, look for teams being led by someone new or a little bit unsure of the position or simply very ambitious within the company who needs to prove himself and needs some henchmen for the job. If a company is going through a reorganisation, volunteer hard for a new role, almost regardless of what it is; this gives you a *great excuse* to reset your performance clock, to redefine your job requirements, to terminate your previous undesirable projects, and to restart your "grace period" for getting acceptably competent at your job. Hang out and network with the B and C students, in and out of the office (just not to the point of overfamiliarity), because they are the ones who can get you onto a team or into a company that (a) would actually take you and (b) is very likely to be run by a B student. Indeed, a B student is an ideal manager for you, a concept that is very important for the mediocre employee to fully embrace. A B-student manager is neither so good that he will require excellence nor so bad that he is likely to be clueless and therefore useless. Look for corporate volatility, and keep moving and changing roles until you find a good spot in which to settle

---

23   In some ways, this is a curse of success. The original Peter Principle states that "every employee in an organisation eventually rises to his level of incompetence." In younger companies, when the founders or original executives attain a certain level of accomplishment and resultant wealth, they become lazy, complacent, or arrogant. And in so doing, senior managers in successful companies eventually rise to their level of *indifference*. They lose motivation to manage well, and the company devolves. I hereby name this the Refractory Peter Principle.

and that puts you at just the right capability layering for your mediocre work style.

One former colleague of mine had a long run of such movements that were particularly effective. Possibly competent at his function, but mediocre in management skills or strategic capability, his job-switching timing was impeccable. He started out as a general member of the finance team in one corporation where I worked. A secondary support function, it nevertheless afforded him access to the managing director and to future strategic plans. He was involved in evaluating the acquisition of a subsidiary that was purchased and incorporated as sister unit. As the founders of that original company had taken the cash and walked, he was in a great position to lobby for and to receive the general managership of that company; he was now one of the only people who knew how that company worked, given his role in the acquisition. He thus gained the helm of a growing, though not profitable, unit. Even though he failed to make it profitable, over the next three years, he was in place as the customer base grew many multiples, mostly thanks to the integration with the mother company. Of course, the subsidiary's profitability was never known externally, because all numbers were rolled up into the public filings of the listed mother company. After a few years as the "head of a growing subsidiary", he parlayed this position into the role of COO at a successful startup that had just obtained major financing and was to receive several more rounds over the next few years, most of which was used to acquire smaller rivals. The early work of developing the startup's brand having already been done before his arrival, he joined at precisely the time that cash was being injected and growth was assured. (Secondary and later funding rounds within startups are actually fantastic opportunities to look for "relaxed oversight" from senior management, as much pressure is lifted and the symptoms of self-satisfaction begin to creep in.[24]) He lasted there about three years, and when the pressure to actually start delivering results through methods other than rival acquisition grew too cumbersome, he left to join a brand-new startup in a senior role, once again finding the volatility of a new and unsure set of founders looking for someone who had the appearance of a "steady, experienced hand". His status as a prime example of a B student was confirmed when I found out that he had recently hired another former colleague of ours whom I had known quite assuredly as a C student.

Remember that this chapter deals with companies that are devolving. That means that many of them generally still have the appearance of success, which, in turn, means that their "numbers" have been "up and to the right"— that is, increasing sales, revenue, profit, active customers, or whatever other relevant metric exists in their particular marketplaces. This environment creates more than enough space for mediocrity to take hold and to flourish, like the rot and rust under the facade of a newly constructed shiny Chinese skyscraper.[25] This ***Growth Curve Camouflage*** **presents a perfect opportunity for the mediocre employee to prosper.** When most company indicators are already increasing, no matter for what reason, even if the company is simply in an organically growing industry or exists during

---

24 An interesting case study of this is the original social network, Friendster. As an article in which the founder, Jonathan Abrams, was interviewed observes: "If the engineering challenges at Friendster were obvious, Abrams was having too much fun to worry. He assumed that with enough money and the right people, the problems would solve themselves." He had just raised $15 million in funding and had hired a panoply of "management talent" from Silicon Valley. Only one word is needed to highlight the result of this attitude and approach and the subsequent failure of the Friendster project: Facebook; Max Chafkin, "How to Kill a Great Idea!" *Inc.*, http://www.inc.com/magazine/20070601/features-how-to-kill-a-great-idea.html (2007).
25 Jessie Jiang, "Not Built to Last: China's Overused Wrecking Ball," *TIME*, http://www.time.com/time/world/article/0,8599,2030548,00.html (2010).

a boom cycle, it becomes very easy to take credit for some of that growth and to mask any personal failures. From a purely logical perspective, correlation does not imply causation (moreover, "presence" does not even imply correlation!): just because you are at the company or doing a project does not mean that you or it had a positive impact on the company. But, with *a priori* growing trend lines, it becomes impossible to split out your contribution from the company's overall success without careful analysis of results. And, the steeper the growth, the less likely anyone in the company will bother to engage in this task! If the number of active customers is growing by 40 percent each year, no one will have the slightest idea whether you contributed 2 to 3 percent of that growth through your own efforts. Even if you fail miserably and actually cost the company 2 percentage points of that growth, the net growth of 38 percent is still incredible and will hardly make anyone less happy or more likely to scrutinise than the 40 percent they would have had you not been involved. And that state of events is true while you are still *at* the company. Later, when interviewing for future jobs outside the company, someone else's ability to accurately evaluate your self-attribution will be completely nil.

The situation would be much different if company growth was only 5 percent. Then your +/–2 percent would be much more carefully evaluated, even though your work, effort, output, and net contribution might be the same in both cases. You will only benefit from the Growth Curve Camouflage when the curve is sufficiently steep. So, look for a company that is already growing, is in a lucky industry, or is even going through a bubble so every action you take looks like a positive success against the backdrop of the success of the whole company. You will be able to claim credit for almost any part of that growth or to mask your own failures. Even if the company is not growing overall, find a metric that looks impressive and "own it". For example, perhaps you can be the one who increases customer satisfaction by 30 percent (maybe by redefining "satisfaction" to exclude reports of previously known problems). In a growing company, it is often up to you to choose your own Camouflage.

In my role as an interviewer, I often see résumés that take responsibility for growing "the user base by 100 percent" or for "increasing revenue by 50 percent"—all very impressive numbers on their own. I have met many candidates who couple such numbers with lofty titles, such as "COO", which they obtained during the Internet bubble cycle of 2000–2001 when companies that would go bust a year later were growing at 500 percent annually and hiring executives by the dozen. The claims of numbers and titles are technically true, of course, and are impossible to question without knowing the specifics of the prior companies. No B-student interviewer will bother to research such trifles when conducting his own hiring. For the mediocre interviewee, the Growth Curve Camouflage is particularly potent in that case.

Earlier in this chapter, the concept of organisational devolution is discussed within a corporation as a whole. It is useful to explore a particular subgenre of this that occurs at the executive management level of a corporation. This is because an *inversion layer* exists inside a typical corporation above which the flying is smooth and steadily upward, but below which there is much turbulence and strife. In climatology, an atmospheric inversion occurs whenever a layer of hot air inverts the normal phenomenon of decreasing temperature with higher altitude. A glider pilot will typically catch a rising thermal, which is a bubble or column of hot air that, being less dense than the cold air above it, will continue to rise until it cools. Unfortunately, an inversion layer will prematurely stop this rise, because the hot air of the layer blocks the rising thermal. Similarly, **the mediocre employee will look for the inversion layer in a corporation and seek to penetrate it as quickly as possible**, perhaps even entering the corporation above the layer to start with, because being located below it for any period of time is almost guaranteed to limit success (the "hot air", in all senses of the phrase, at the inversion layer will block your upward rise!).

How is it possible to spot where this layer begins? Look for the management layer at which senior managers will seek to avoid rating their subordinates poorly. Above a certain level of manager, to do so would be evidence of their gross incompetence in their primary responsibility—building a good team. This applies to C-level executives and often VPs and sometimes directors. Lower-ranked managers can still rate subordinates poorly, because they are themselves often still measured on lots of other criteria (or they simply do not know the inversion rule yet!). But, what self-respecting CEO would rate any of his ten VPs as "not meeting expectations"? After all, the CEO probably hired the VP, put the VP in charge of a function, and has been instructing the VP directly. Too many publicly failing VPs will make the CEO start to look bad himself. With a delusion of superiority also being the norm, the CEO will often be confident that *"anyone who works for me* must *be good"*. On top of which, it has been scientifically shown that people already in a position of power, such as the VP in question, lie more easily and effectively[26] and know very well how to cover their asses; this further reduces the likelihood of getting a negative performance evaluation from the CEO. At the end of all this, even if there is any perceived failure on the part of the VP, it will be dealt with behind the scenes,

26   Dana Carney, "Defend Your Research: Powerful People are Better Liars," *Harvard Business Review,* http://hbr.org/2010/05/defend-your-research-pow-erful-people-are-better-liars/ar/1 (2010).

or perhaps during salary raise time, or perhaps via a very, very slow squeeze out of the company. This squeeze will take many years, because a VP who departs soon after joining the executive team, again, makes the CEO look bad. This also marks yet another way to identify the location of the inversion layer: above it, employees stay around for many years in relatively fixed roles. In positions immediately below it, it is typical to see huge employee churn and very short tenures in the company.

Yet, none of this dynamic will be obviously evident to anybody but top insiders, and definitely not to potential future employers of someone like the hypothetical VP. In this way, the executive layer of a corporation continually protects and reinforces itself in a bubble above the inversion layer. Meanwhile, this top management as a class gets fed fat raises and self-rewards from the company till. Just like investment bankers do for their bonuses, executives convince themselves they are great and are worth it and so must be anyone working for them. The only limitation to this bubble might come from the board of directors, but in corporations, they are more often part of the same bubble and subject to the same dynamics than an arm's length scrutiniser on executive performance. And so, Western corporations have an environment in which executive compensation grew 25 percent in 2010 and is proportionally higher relative to employee compensation than at any time since the Victorian era.[27] Executive self-satisfaction and self-perception of infallibility are the chief explanations for this rise in absurd compensation *and the primary cause of corporate devolution.*

It is very difficult to rise above the inversion layer if the mediocre employee does not do so very quickly upon

---

27   Graham Snowdon, "Pay gap widening to Victorian levels," *The Guardian*, http://www.guardian.co.uk/business/2011/may/16/high-pay-commission-wage-disparity (2010).

joining the company. The more time he spends below it, the more mistakes he will make and the more enemies he will accumulate, simply as a natural function of time. Remember that, as is explained previously in this book, five friends and zero enemies are much more preferable than ten friends and one enemy when it comes time for the promotion committee to meet. Once an executive above the inversion layer decides he does not like you, he will fight tooth and nail never to have you rise above it, if only as a point of pride, and your success at the company will be limited. This is why most senior executives in corporations have not worked their way up through the ranks but instead are hired externally. (Exceptions are always notable and prove the rule.[28]) If possible, then, the mediocre employee will try to be hired directly above the inversion layer, even if it means joining a smaller company or subsidiary. If you cannot achieve this, at least try to report to someone already *inside* this layer, because she is less likely to want to tell her own manager about the fact that she has a lot of poor performers on her team and will want to help you help her look good. If you do find yourself below the inversion layer for more than several years, it is time to change roles or even companies, provided you can take a step up to get closer to the layer. Once you do get above the layer: welcome to nirvana, because your career success is basically guaranteed, regardless of your mediocrity! Like numerous failed CEOs who get hired over and over,[29] you, too, can count on a long, fruitful, and scrutiny-free cruise to retirement.

👍 👍 👍

28   A. T. Kearney, "'Home-Grown' CEO," http://www.atkearney.com/index.php/Publications/qhome-grownq-ceo.html (2011).
29   Carmen Nobel, "Failure *Is* an Option," *Portfolio.com*, http://www.portfolio.com/executives/features/2008/10/05/Why-Failed-CEOs-Get-Rehired/ (2008).

Now practice some of the concepts from the chapter in this pop quiz. The chart shows the lifecycle of a smaller corporation, such as a midsize startup as it goes through different stages of maturity. Answer the questions below based on the data in the chart:

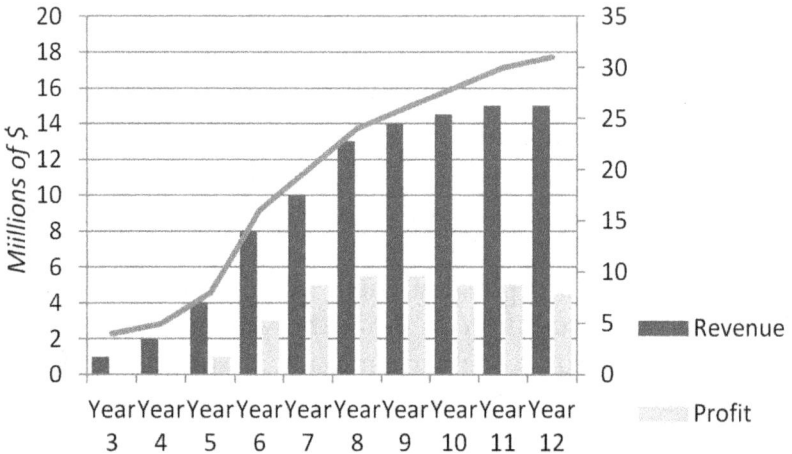

Question 1: What is a great time for a mediocre employee to join the company? Year _____

Question 2: Assuming the mediocre employee joined in Year 8, what is a great time for him to leave the company? Year

_____

Question 3: For this employee who joined in Year 8 and is now leaving, how should he update his résumé for maximum benefit?

- Contributed to growth of _____% in _____ *(metric 1)*_____.

- Managed initiatives that helped increase _____ *(metric 2)*_____ by $_____ in ___ years.

- Maintained _____ *(metric 3)*_____ above 30% on growing revenues.

Answers:

1: Any answer between Year 5 to 8 is acceptable. Before this, the company is still working very hard, and the executives are probably still very attentive and micromanaging. After this, the company has almost peaked and is close to beginning its devolution, which is evident in the sinking profitability, even as customers grow (an indicator of poor long-term investment and brand building).

Bonus correct answer: Year 3. You might just be able to get in above the inversion layer and onto the executive team while the company is still small (if you are lucky or have the right connections).

2: Year 9 or 10. After this, very few metrics remain to be claimed for résumé padding. Also, staying much longer beyond this will likely result in career paralysis, because the company is likely becoming stable and volatility disappears. The only exception may be if the company starts to try to "reorganise" every twelve months along new team structures, which may still present some opportunity to move from team to team.

3: The correct, and truthful, points to add to a résumé for an employee who joins in Year 8 and leaves in Year 10 are filled in:

- Contributed to growth of __15__ % in __the Active Customer Base__ .

- Managed initiatives that helped increase ___ __Revenue__ by $__1.5M__ in _2_ years.

- Maintained __Profit Margin__ above 30% on growing revenues.

CHAPTER 8
Female Prerogatives

We fortunately no longer live in a world where women are relegated to the typing pool or get hired just to make it easier for the boss to have an affair without leaving the office (perhaps J. Pierrepont Finch would not have had nearly as much success had *How to Succeed in Business Without Really Trying* been set today and he had faced double the competition). Women have by now nearly achieved as much opportunity and success in the corporate world as men, which in no way makes it less likely to find mediocre employees within the female cohort as it does amongst their male colleagues. It may even be possible that a higher proportion of mediocrity exists amongst women: the residual societal misogyny that limits the advancement of women may by now be *significantly outweighed* by the additional "boost" that *mediocre* female employees have by exercising some of the powerful tactics in this chapter. Although the analysis of comparative statistics is beyond the scope of this book, if you are such a woman, this chapter illuminates certain special things that only someone like you can do to gain this very boost.

Now, the mediocre reader, skimming through this chapter, might perceive it to be "sexist" or have some other negative reaction that springs to the mind of a semi-reflective reader. This reader should be assured that the intention herein is quite the opposite: women are *just as capable of being mediocre as men*. No lack or deficiency whatsoever in their skills, capacity, or determination is implied. The chapter simply adds more tools to their tool belts for achieving success (perhaps thereby even giving them more of the unfair advantage referenced above). Why be greedy when distributing tools of the trade?

In previous chapters, the issue of working on "the right" projects or tasks is addressed. The female tool belt includes a very strong tool to facilitate this: **claim inability**. More precisely: when being asked to work on a *wrong* project or task, it is often possible to declare that you do not know how to do a particular functional part of that project, have never done it before, do not have the skill required, or are afraid that you would not be able to do it up to standard, and so forth. Often, if your boss or task manager is a man (or even sometimes a woman), do not be surprised to find that the response is, "Oh, okay. I guess you can work on this other project then". Your claim of inability will be even more effective when accompanied by a wide-eyed, blinking look that says, "I couldn't possibly begin to understand this before you need it completed". In the rare case that the response to you is instead, "Well, I expect you to know how to do this", you can always flip this immediately to your favour by saying that yes, of course, you will surely figure it out, or take the appropriate coursework, or get trained by a knowledgeable person, A.S.A.P. Do not forget to also note this effort on your next performance review to show how dedicated you are to your job and how much you have learned and progressed.

If you find yourself still unduly burdened by tasks that require actual work or unacceptable effort, such as learning something new, a mediocre female employee still has one more powerful backup tactic. Do not be afraid to ask colleagues or subordinates, especially men, to do things that you would not (or cannot) do yourself. Often, men have a psychological barrier known as "pride", "ego", and so forth that prevents them from asking others to do something they are not prepared to do themselves, but women can opt to ignore this with relative impunity. This is an area where men's psychology can be used to your advantage. Consider that Joan of Arc personally did very little (actually: none at all) cutting and thrusting during her epic battles. Although she wore armour, she was not capable of actual hand-to-hand combat, instead letting the thousands of men who followed her do that rather dangerous work. On the other hand, even to this day, soldiers would find it hard to follow into battle a *male* who is not prepared to pick up a gun, yell "hooah!" and unload a clip at the enemy (officially, even ranks up to colonel are expected to be in the front lines).

In the slightly less-combat-oriented corporate world, the mediocre female employee can still avoid many tasks via such **selective defensive delegation**. The key is to think about how you can use the other person's ego, gentlemanliness, insecurity, and so forth to your advantage. Just remember to explain your request as something you are not *capable* of doing rather than something you do not *want* to do. The following chart shows some real-world examples:

Statement	Implicit inability you are claiming	Targeted psychological lever
"Can you do this Net Present Value calculation? I'm not really sure how to do it right."	Lack of knowledge in a difficult methodology	Pride in being able to handle complex and difficult things
"Can you talk to Jim about extending the deadline for our project? I'm really afraid he's going to yell at me if I ask him."	Fear of dealing with conflict	Personal ego boost by providing a service to a fearful colleague
"Could you organise this meeting for twenty people? You're just much better at getting everyone on board."	Inability to get commitment from a big group	Insecurity about own ability to get commitment must be demonstrably overcome
"I'm exhausted and can't think straight anymore. I just have to go home. Is it okay if you finish this tonight on your own?"	Physical weakness	Pride in being strong and capable of working all night if necessary

Not every mediocre female employee is endowed with the skills for such psychological manipulation. Some may instead opt for visual manipulation. Although this sounds difficult to accomplish, what it really comes down to is nothing more than **wear sexy clothing**. This is simply another way to be "interesting" to colleagues (as mandated in Chapter 4) without revealing too much about yourself or even having to be conversational or funny. By this point in Western society, sexy dress is largely a riskless act in Western corporations. Tendencies towards sexually harassing or challenging *acts* have effectively been "beaten out" of male employees through employee training,[30] legal liability threats, and

---

30   Tina Fey says in her book *Bossypants* (2011) that she has sat through fourteen sexual harassment seminars at NBC; cited in Katie Roiphe, "Tina Fey's Tough Girl Feminism," *Slate*, http://www.slate.com/id/2289892/ (2011).

growing female prevalence in the workforce. But they will never be able to exterminate *desire* (if they ever succeed, the human race will die out for lack of procreation). For a female employee, dressing in a sexy way is a very potent way of passively triggering this desire and using its effect to her advantage. It is known that men are generally visually stimulated, and it is also pretty well-proven that they are always more compliant, malleable, and agreeable when dealing with a woman who, even if not strictly good-looking, at least *wants to please* through what she is wearing. Her choice of sexy clothing communicates, *"I could have worn something average and nonenticing, but I* chose *this today, knowing that you would look at it and that it would positively stimulate your eye and gratify your visual desire."* It is a very subtle gesture of "gifting" a type of pleasure, but because it requires no reciprocation (for that matter, an attempt to do so, such as a compliment, would usually be condemned as harassment), it can be executed without any acknowledgement and with full and utter deniability of intent.

A female employee can usually greatly increase her standing in her corporation in this way—simply by wearing sexy clothing. This method can be used as effectively by good and bad employees, too; it is not restricted to the mediocre, so it is important not to correlate sexy clothing with mediocrity. The method has nothing to do with job performance, skill, or accomplishment, but if you are a mediocre female employee, you do not really care about these things (see the definition of "mediocre" in the Introduction); this is why you should feel free to actively engage in the exploitation of this method! You will have an easier time getting other people to do things for you, get more positive evaluations of your own performance from most men and some women, sell more if you are in a Sales role, and wield certain advantages of being a female without having any obligation to submit yourself to the downsides. And if somebody questions your overly sexy wardrobe, you may just have a goldmine of legal payouts on your hands[31] (which could be considered a form of corporate success, in its own way).

One personal example that I remember fondly is that of a business school classmate of mine. She was an Eastern European woman, of very modest skills and intelligence, but above-average height, figure, and tightness of clothing. She was offered what was at the time an extremely coveted job at one of the larger global investment banks. Competition was fierce for those positions, as they were very well-paid and in an industry that had not yet fully disgraced itself.[32] The amusing part of this story is that despite the fact that she was only one of three people who *failed* the programme (putting her in the bottom 0.3 percent of the class), her benevolent employer saw it in his heart to hold the offer open for her while she took an extra semester to pass her failed courses. Of course, no one in my class had any doubt of what her employer expected that she would bring to the table.

Lastly, one very potent tactic of the mediocre works extremely well, but only if the actor is obviously a woman—**act very caring and motherly.** To execute this, extensively

---

31   Debrahlee Lorenzana was fired from Citibank in 2010 for dressing too provocatively; whether her goldmine will pay off remains to be seen after the courts rule; Courtney Comstock, "Woman Says Citibank Fired Her Because She Was Too Hot," *Business Insider*, http://www.businessinsider.com/debrahlee-lorenzana-citi-2010-6 (2010).

32   Besides being responsible for the Global Financial Crisis, exorbitant executive pay, and various other sins, the finance and especially investment banking domains are still probably the few remaining ones in which sexual "harassment tendencies" have not yet been beaten out of the system. The entire industry is a well-known bastion of sexism; see, for example, Kyle Stock, "Casualties of the Crisis: Stress, Sexism and Layoffs Thin the Ranks of Women on Wall Street," *Fins Finance*, http://www.fins.com/Finance/Articles/SB128317950058932491/Casualties-of-the-Crisis-Stress-Sexism-and-Layoffs-Thin-the-Ranks-of-Women-on-Wall-Street (2010).

verbalise sentiments of *compassion* ("Oh, I'm so sorry to hear about your stomach virus—you must have had a horrible night, I really feel for you"), *service* ("I'm running down to the canteen—can I get you anything? You haven't even had lunch today yet, you poor thing"), *self-sacrifice* ("I'll use my own biweekly one-to-one time with our boss to talk about how helpful you've been to our project, because it's that important for him to know"), *unflappable cheerleading* ("I know the boss didn't like the strategy you presented at the meeting, but I know you've got great ideas and you're going to do so well next time! You're just so good at this stuff"), *comfort providing* ("Is it too hot in here? Can I turn it down for you?"), and other things you can say in a similar vein as if you were pretending to be the colleague's mother. Furthermore, *make promises to take care of things* for your target ("I'll see if our boss can do anything about . . .", or "I'll talk to HR about . . .", or "I'll work to get our team some . . .", or "I'll try to take care of this when I get some extra time . . ."). These comments actually place no obligation on you to follow through, but the perception of colleagues will be that you are going to one day and that your efforts are generally directed towards their benefit. And never let up the acting—keep pressing the motherliness (it requires remarkably little effort, once you get into the mind-set). You will avoid many confrontations and will often be given huge benefits of the doubt. *It is hard to argue, to contradict, or to even think ill of someone who is constantly saying to your face that she is trying to help you.*[33]

I once had a manager who was the model of a caring mother hen, always clucking about how much she was advocating for us and trying to improve our team's lot, without ever actually sticking her neck out or putting herself on the line in the least (something that was obvious in any meeting in

---

[33] This observation also holds true for male employees, although it is often much harder for them to repeatedly pull it off without irony or self-doubt.

which I had the chance to actually hear the substance of what she communicated to senior management). It always took a few quarters for her direct reports to catch on, however, by which time the company had reorganised again, one or the other party had moved teams, or some other thing had happened to make the whole issue moot, and she could move on to mothering another batch of ignorant chicks. I nodded in profound, almost earnest, sympathy as she once explained to me how she fought so very hard to get me an extra 1.2 percent on top of a 2.4 percent annual raise (during a cycle in which I "exceeded expectations", as she herself acknowledged via her signature in my *a priori* worthless performance review).

👍 👍 👍

I have, in this book, refrained from giving any identifying names either of people or of companies in my personal anecdotes and consequently cannot give any details that would further illustrate the above examples of female prerogatives. Instead, here is a table showing the utilisation of the described tactics by my female colleagues in the aggregate of my entire corporate career. If the numbers seem high to the reader, consider it less a commentary on women in the workplace and more of a testimony that *mediocrity* in general is more common than you might want to think:

Tactic	% of female colleagues who use it at least occasionally
Claiming inability to do a task	25%
accompanied by a wide-eyed, blinking stare	15%
Using selective defensive delegation by asking someone else to do something you do not want to do	70%
Wearing sexy clothes	35%
Acting caring and motherly	20%

As a final note for men who are reading this chapter: it is strongly suggested that you do **not** employ any of the methods described herein. You may be laughed out of the company, fired for incompetence, or typecast as a whiny queen. You have been warned.

Conclusion

John Johnson ran out of the subway station, trying to cut the corners of all the obstacles in his way. This was not the first time he was late for the weekly team meeting, and he knew the precise places to put his feet and even the angles to turn his body to minimise the time from the station to the office door. *Plant left foot to the right of that mailbox, turn body 45 degrees left, next step off the curb.* The practiced mechanics of his motion left his mind free to think about what he was going to say to excuse his lateness. Well, he certainly was not going to acknowledge the fault, nor let anyone mention it. He needed to whack that mole before it even popped its head; he knew giving his lateness a positive spin would probably result in its being forgotten within a few minutes. "Alright", he figured, "I've got it". He usually didn't like being one of those "late-night work" heroes, because it might raise undue expectations for future late-night work; he preferred to be a "lunchtime" hero who did miracles of effort during the workday, turning Quick Wins around before the day was out. In this case, though, he would go out on a limb and say, "I was up very late last night checking the numbers from our marketing campaign in the analytics tool, because I wanted a full week of data for today's presentation due in to the head office. One of the metrics was out of whack, so I was e-mailing back and forth with analytics customer support, trying to resolve the discrepancy. We finally got there at 1:00 a.m., so I'm a bit late this morning". Who is going to argue with that?

And he was right, no one did. There were some semi-impressed nods from a few of the folks in his department (they were of the type of solid corporate functionary who could rarely vocalise coherent ideas themselves but would instead often signal enthusiastic participation via gesticulation or facial expressions), and his boss, anxious to take control back and do some talking of his own, nodded and moved on. His boss was from the really old school of Operators, back from when the nice lady at the end of the phone line would repeat your instructions and sometimes even your message to the receiving end, lest something get lost over the poor connection. So, too, did John Johnson's boss like to take any worthwhile comment made by anyone in the room, reshape it into his own words, subtly add in a dose of his own contribution should the cause be a good one, and then release it back into the wild for everyone to hear the now-tamed, and personally appropriated, comment. What made this style particularly effective, John Johnson reflected, was the complete conviction and certainty that his boss used whenever issuing his processed output; it was as though the thing was already decided and done and his boss had been thinking about it for weeks. His boss's steely resolve and disregard for possibly being proven wrong by facts later was impressive. Of course, about eight out of ten of such pronouncements did end up having to be eventually altered or sometimes entirely discarded when their errors became obvious, and his batting average of 0.200 would have put any corporate pitcher to shame, but, here, too, his boss was very good at keeping everyone's focus on the two out of ten that he got right. Had anyone asked him, he would have, with a straight face, claimed a batting average of 1.000. So, when a topic came up about which there was not much for his boss to say or much gain to be had, his boss was, for once, very happy to get back to the formal agenda. John Johnson generally carefully studied these traits of his boss in a most observant manner (evidently, they were leading to success), but today, he was glad that his boss was going to let the issue of lateness get lost in the ether.

In this weekly team meeting, the tradition was to go around the room and for each member to discuss the project he or she was working on that week and the progress that had been made—standard stuff, and mostly serving the purpose of keeping his boss informed of what everyone on the team was doing. Usually, this was the only dialogue his boss had with most team members during the week, as the boss had started, over the last few quarters, to spend more and more time on the executive floor. The reason became clear recently when it was announced that his boss was getting promoted. Even though his boss had manifestly lost interest in the performance of the team and its results and had even stopped responding to e-mail, he needed to keep a lid on things so they did not fall apart completely and so no bad news floated up before he made the official move upstairs. John Johnson was quite happy with this state of events and the once-a-week review, as it meant he had a good public forum to tout his own accomplishments while avoiding the scrutiny of a deeply involved manager. There was at least six more months of "making up the numbers" ahead of him to look forward to (and the new boss would likely take at least another three months to make sense of it all!). As for what the actual departmental results were, even John Johnson had lost track of it a few months ago when his boss stopped pressuring the analytics team for accurate monthly reports. They were waiting for new management, same as John Johnson.

It was Suzi's turn to talk. This was always a moment of anticipation and dread, both of which were the result of the predictable gibberish that would emanate from Suzi's mouth for at least the next five minutes. It was always amusing to hear how she could go on talking in platitudes or empty declarations, saying things that sounded grammatical at least but had little meaning and even less impact on the company. Dreadful and cringeworthy, too. But this was her signature style, and, having been recently laterally promoted (albeit into a role that no one wanted and that had no mandate but that she had seized like a Rottweiler), she must have thought that her vocalisations were effective and redoubled her efforts. Heck, it might even work again on John Jonson's boss, because he was happy to take things at face value these days, given his impending move.

"I'm really glad that our team has an opportunity to work on this great project, and I'm thrilled to be leading it", Suzi enthused. "It can really change the performance of the company and our product line. And we have to make it have a positive impact on our customer retention, because it will help our marketing and customer service teams collaborate. Increased collaboration is always good, and we need to make it work, and I'm working really hard to connect the two groups in an efficient manner. We can make sure that issues that arise in one are dealt with quickly in the other, and vice versa. I'm looking at the best way to do this, and I'm going to rely on all your help, but I am just a conduit and it won't work without you. I'll give you all the support you need, and I'd like your support as well. Let me know what problems you have and what needs to be solved. But I really enjoy working with all of you, so it will be great. . . ."

These phrases, while studiously avoiding making her responsible for any course of action or executing any actual work, made her appear enthusiastic, involved, and committed. Committed to something. Committed to commitment, at least. At the end of the day, though, for as long as John Johnson had known her in the company, she did no work of any consequence, knew nothing of any depth, and inspired no one of any relevancy. John Johnson was starting to suspect that Suzi did not even qualify as mediocre. Still, he would himself give the phrase *"I'm really thrilled to be working on this project"* a go at the nearest opportunity.

While Suzi was exposing her innermost feelings of commitment, John Johnson drifted off into fantasyland. He wondered if his boss was getting promoted above the inversion layer. John Johnson had seen how the senior VPs changed demeanour once they were promoted to that level. They rather quickly stopped having one-on-one conversations with their former team members or any employees, for that matter, and would rarely thereafter appear on his floor at all. When he did see them, usually in groups of two or three, they would often exchange knowing looks with each other, and John Johnson swore he could sometimes detect a mutual wink and a nod. They would issue wise pronouncements once a quarter at some all-hands meeting, but what they did apart from this, John Johnson really had no idea. He knew it could not involve actually making *difficult* decisions, because, for a decision to be "difficult", some conflict must exist in choosing one path or the other. But conflict can only arise whenever the different paths are informed by actual information that highlights tradeoffs. And, because he knew how much information was flowing up to that level, at least about the marketing end of things, because he *himself* was responsible for producing and distributing that information, he knew that the SVPs did not have anywhere near enough information for most of their decisions to be considered "difficult" in any fact-based sense of the word. Well, he figured, they must be making a lot of "easy" decisions, then. "That's the life, up in the clouds!" he thought—easy decision making, surreptitious backslapping, and self-awarded bonuses. His boss had likely been granted his first access to this golden goose, as he was soon going to report to the SVP of marketing.

It was soon John Johnson's turn to talk, and he willed himself back into the early-morning caffeine-fuelled reality of the meeting. He briefly described the progress he was making with the quarterly presentation summarising the marketing department's key metrics. It was going really well; last night's activities helped him get the latest numbers included; he had developed a new format for displaying revenue growth trending; the market research team was finally cooperating and providing support. But, the density of positivity could not overcome one fact that John Johnson was dreading and was trying to postpone reckoning with by eating up the rest of the meeting's available time: the fact that the presentation was a week late. His boss brought this up, with a well-placed interjection. Even though he was hoping not to have this fact mentioned publicly, John Johnson had a reply already prepared, behind the breakable emergency cover-your-ass glass: "After the great suggestion you made last week regarding changing the trend-line average to a seven-day window from the thirty-day window, I wanted to make sure all the data from all the other departments had enough granularity to display properly. It was a really good idea and gives the report much more clarity." Boom. One stone. Two birds. Not only was he pointing out his own initiative in making the report better and collaborating with other teams, but he was able to include a nongratuitous compliment of his boss. He could see the boss's pleased expression, even as the boss pressed on, "So, when will it be done?" John Johnson replied, "By the end of the day—in your inbox." And the matter was closed. John Johnson hoped his boss would remember compliments like this when the salary review committee got in touch with him six months down the line and asked him for a thirty-second opinion on whether John Johnson should get promoted. By that time, his boss would no longer be doing the performance review, with his replacement formally responsible for it, but, of course, no one would read the performance review of a manager who had known the team only for a few weeks. So, John Johnson needed to have his current boss be his advocate in the ranks of the executives for a long time to come.

At the end of the meeting, the issue of hiring a junior associate for the department came up. John Johnson's boss told the team he was going to get HR to coordinate this but asked for a volunteer to liaise with them. At the word "volunteer", John Johnson's mind kicked into gear with a well-practiced programmed response: what's in it for me? how difficult is it? how visible is it? His mind was made up even before the third of these was answered. Waiting a single courtesy beat (volunteering too quickly was considered bad form and an indication of brown-nosing) and then immediately raising his hand before anyone else got theirs off the table, John Johnson said, "I'll be glad to do it." He had instantly recognised that it was a great opportunity (a) to volunteer and to be noticed right then and there and (b) to be in control of the future employee's character and eventual loyalty. It would also give him a chance to get additional contact with other senior managers required for interviewing and hiring approval, thereby helping him increase his visibility throughout the company. As he was concluding these mental gymnastics, a final brilliant thought illuminated him: "But, let me coordinate it directly myself, and I'll just keep HR in the loop", he added. He had remembered that last time HR was involved in hiring for his team, it took six months, and there were a whole host of other delays and busy work with paperwork, approvals, reviews, lost forms, and so forth. Two candidates had simply gotten tired of waiting for HR to process the job offer. His boss, having been exposed to the same problems on more than one occasion, was sympathetic and agreed to this condition and to John Johnson's leading the assignment. His boss thanked him for volunteering (in his own way, of course: "This is a difficult position to fill given how quickly we need it. John will take this on directly, and will keep HR aware of the progress. Decided.") and dismissed the meeting.

John Johnson had two more meetings before lunch. One was a planning meeting for the quarterly strategic review to be delivered to the bigwigs from headquarters who rolled into town for a full day of listening (and a few minutes of their own talking, which was all they could generate after only a single day's exposure to an entire regional strategy). The other meeting was a mandatory HR Q&A about the new pension provider the company had recently chosen. He could never figure out the point of these Q&A sessions, because HR never knew anything more than what was already written in the official documentation and that anyone more senior than a mail clerk at his company could pretty much figure out. But, oh well, the HR director was to be there, so John Johnson needed to show up and say what a great idea the new pension plan was and how it would really benefit employee retention. The HR director was so disdained by the staff for his useless meddling and general overall cluelessness (even about things like employee policies) that he rarely got any support from anyone. He had become director when his predecessor moved to a subsidiary company and senior management was too busy (or, more likely, too indifferent) to spend a lot of time recruiting a new HR director; he was the most senior person in the queue and got the job by default. Which is why he appreciated John Johnson that much more, because John Johnson had recently made it a point to compliment him on various and sundry things without putting upon him any further responsibilities beyond those of saying "thank you" and graciously smiling. John Johnson had the sense that the HR director preferred being liked to being respected. In any case, by virtue of being a director, he was on the promotion committee, and John Johnson knew well it never hurt to have more friends at that precious director level. Well, at least he would have some more mental strategising time while he sat through the mandatory meeting.

Afterwards, John Johnson took a detour on his way back to dropping off his laptop at his desk before lunch. All these HR thoughts had reminded him of someone he needed to see with whom he had not chatted for a while: the HR team admin. It was not because she was one of the better-looking girls in the office and always dressed in such a way as to remind everyone of it. John Johnson knew that any hint of an office relationship or even an attempt at the same would cause a lot of talk about a lot of things about which a lot of people would attempt to get familiar. And familiarity with his office mates was definitely not on his agenda, for he knew where that could lead. In the same way, he knew that he could never look at Bob from accounting with respect again, after Bob told him about his embarrassing gastrointestinal problems at the last company Christmas party, grabbing his arm and drooling a confession just as John Johnson was on the way out the door. And John Johnson did not want to see the HR admin because he needed something from her. In fact, she was a little bit useless, as he had been convinced in previous conversations with her in which she would never know the answer to his questions, would promise to get back to him, and would never do so. Though, she was quite ambitious, as John Johnson surmised by the way she never said no and always acted very concerned about any issues he brought up. (Not that it stopped her from forgetting them the minute he stepped away!) No, John Johnson wanted to see the HR admin because HR admins *know things*, like who is getting promoted, how big the bonus pool is, and all sorts of other useful tidbits. A few minutes' chat with her, and John Johnson might have a bit better idea of where to apply his upcoming corporate efforts. Besides, he would get to see which of the VPs were around this week, because they sat in the adjacent office section.

After the quick chitchat (during which he always practiced injecting a bit of his dry wit), John Johnson dropped off his laptop and headed to lunch. He had no intention of leaving the office today, even though a few of his teammates had asked him if he wanted to step out for dim sum. It was his general policy to eat at the company cafeteria, as spending an hour out with his peers was fun but would not get him anywhere, because none of them were going to tell his boss anything his boss did not already know. And right now, he needed to increase his personal propaganda with the senior managers in the company in preparation for the upcoming performance review cycle. Besides, he did not feel like talking about his latest paragliding achievements or his upcoming vacation to Australia yet again. He was running out of jokes about getting eaten by sharks and did not have the energy to be interesting today after his chat with the HR admin.

At the company cafeteria, he would always immediately look around the room to see which important people were there, making sure to pretend he had not seen his boss if he was already in the room. One thing John Johnson did not need was another half-hour face-to-face with his boss, during which he had a tendency to start getting into the details of John Johnson's projects—less because his boss was interested in the details and more just to see if he could get John Johnson to squirm. This was another signature style of his boss—making others uncomfortable while retaining mastery of the situation. John Johnson had learned after a few times to simply avoid these sit-downs. Other senior managers were often eating in the canteen (they generally did not go out for lunch like staff due to their full days of meetings), and John Johnson had successfully lunched with many of them by now. VPs even occasionally showed up there, and at least half the regional VPs even knew John Johnson by name now. Today, he was in luck. He saw Simon, the director of Sales, at the sandwich counter and quickly got in the queue behind him.

Simon was alone and was glad for some sandwich company. John Johnson's mind was already deep in preparation as he was ordering his BLT regarding what he would talk about when they sat down. First, he wanted to be looked upon as interesting, so he decided to lead off with something personal but not too intimate, like his trip to Australia! Simon had not heard John Johnson's getting eaten by sharks jokes yet. Jackpot. Then, John Johnson would talk about the big trip he was taking to headquarters and the "really important" project (really just another training session with product development on the new product line) he would be working on while he was there. Perfect.

But John Johnson never got to that, because, after his first Australian shark joke, Simon started talking about his own latest marketing initiative. John Johnson knew he had just hit pay dirt. The more Simon talked, and evidently he did *love* to talk about his projects, the more John Johnson knowingly nodded and asked probing questions. He listened carefully, especially trying to identify what Simon was trying to gain with this project in terms of visible impact or other things he could claim to have achieved. By the end of lunch, Simon had actually started to tell him specifically what positioning messages he would be giving to which VPs, in a hushed, confidential tone. John Johnson could tell that beneath Simon's all-business, wide-smiling, mid-range suit-wearing, generic gold wedding ring-bound exterior was a practiced operator just looking for the next Quick Win. Finally, Simon looked appreciatively at John Johnson, smiled, and said, "Hey, I think you *get* it. We should work together at some point." That was a golden nugget gift of personal propaganda that John Johnson would be sure to mention to his boss as soon as possible, if Simon did not. This was a good lunch, with good results.

John Johnson, with belly and ego sated for the day, headed back to his desk, as it was now time to do the day's work. It was 1:00 p.m., and besides two more meetings this afternoon, he had the rest of the day free. He needed to do the presentation summarising the quarterly marketing figures, metrics, and progress. This was the same report that he had successfully repositioned at the team meeting earlier, but now there was no more procrastination: he had committed in front of everyone that morning to deliver it today. He assumed a proper posture in his chair, feet flat, elbows at 90 degrees, and began to type away. He actually enjoyed, on occasion, utilising his knowledge and skills to produce well-formed decks and colourful, structured slides. This type of work was a bit of diversion and actually somewhat easier than the corporate strategising he found himself carrying out most of the rest of the day. He smiled to himself as he got into the groove.

There was one special slide that required a pivot table manipulation of the data. John Johnson looked at the clock: the time had really flown! There was still one more meeting left that day, and with the meeting he had just gotten back from, only thirty minutes remained in which to finish the presentation. Knowing his teammates, and expecting little success from what he was about to do, he thought he would take a gamble. He walked over to Joanne a few desks over and asked her for help in his most friendly, charming voice. But she was not a corporate neophyte herself: she just stared at him with a look of earnest respect and said, "I've really never done a pivot table before. Can you explain it? I know you're the biggest expert around here." Stopped cold by such an insurmountable (in light of his proximate deadline) repulse, John Johnson had no choice but to say, "Of course, I'll be glad to show you tomorrow. I have to run and finish this deck right now, though", and walk back to his desk. He promised himself to treat Joanne with more competitive regard, henceforth.

Well, it seemed that he was not going to get everything precisely the way he wanted in the deck, but his default fallback was to "massage" the numbers and at least approximate the general trend he was hoping to demonstrate for the customer acquisition figures, especially since the trend needed to appear favourable to the new customer growth project he himself had been leading for the past six months. Even though sometimes John Johnson felt that writing these decks was dogsbody work, he realised it gave him precisely the opportunity to position his own work to the executives in a very positive way. He knew that the analytics system was pretty complicated, and it was doubtful anyone would look at it with the same attention he did. Moreover, he knew the executives who viewed this report only glanced at the summary numbers for about ten minutes and had never yet asked any questions about the input data. Finally, he figured that, with his boss departing soon, the only eye that had an interest in the consistency and accuracy of the numbers, and any way to ascertain the same, was already trained elsewhere. He did a little interpolation of the data here, a little approximate averaging there, and—voilà! The deck was finished.

John Johnson stood up with self-satisfaction, executed "Send" in his e-mail program with a loud thump of the "Enter" key, and headed over to his boss's office to personally follow up with the good news. As he strolled over, he took a mental tally of the time he had spent working that day: two hours and thirty minutes doing actual work (out of eight hours total). Pretty high compared to an average day, actually. He did not feel tired at all, because he had been getting more efficient at navigating the corporation and expending less energy doing so. He had done a good day's work and had probably increased his stature in several ways on this particular day. Although he did wish he did not need to spend so much time in long-winded, stuffy meetings. At his company, they called it "getting consensus" or "group decision making", but he knew that most decisions were made by managers or executives outside these meetings. The meetings were simply a way of getting everybody hitched up to the train that was going the way the rails were pointed anyway. That way, there were no surprises, and everyone had gotten a chance to speak up and to be ignored equally. Still, meetings were an opportunity for him to raise his visibility and to observe effective behaviours of his boss and others.

Not at all like Chris, John Johnson thought as he walked by Chris's desk and silently nodded to him with a smile. Chris was rarely invited to meetings and was a quiet type. John Johnson figured Chris probably did about six to seven hours of real work a day, and his work was actually pretty good. John Johnson had once been very impressed as he flipped through the analysis and the marketing plan Chris had put together as John Jonson was incorporating it into one of his presentations (and on which he put his name as the lead author, of course). But Chris was too conscientious and too focused on doing his job well to pay attention to what really mattered. He did not spend nearly enough time blowing his own horn or making himself appear important. Too bad for Chris, John Johnson thought. He certainly was not going to ruin Chris's fantasy existence in corporate-land.

Popping his head through the open door of the office, John Johnson caught his boss's eye, gave a thumbs up, and said, "It's finished. In your inbox." As his boss nodded in acknowledgement, John Johnson added, with a no-nonsense look, "The customer acquisition numbers came out real well too. Looks like the work I did last month paid off." His boss replied with a brisk "good job", and John Johnson took that as permission to leave. He turned out of the doorway and, walking away, congratulated himself for a job well done.

👍   👍   👍

John Johnson strolled through the office on his way back to his desk. This was the time of day he loved: everyone was starting to pack up to go home, and it was natural to stop doing work and chat with people on the way out. In his office, after 6:00 p.m., no one could reasonably expect anything to be completed that day, so he knew he was safe from text chats from his boss or from *ad hoc* meeting requests. (Timing his responses to these was always a little stressful, even though he had established a general rule of thumb—two-hour delay. But still, he did not like setting these mental timers each time.) He plopped down in his chair and checked his online stock portfolio. Then, leaning back, he opened up his file drawer. It was really a junk drawer, because he had no idea what any of those files in there referred to or why he even filed them anymore; all those projects were so "last quarter". He pulled out a little book with a corporate-looking, high-achievement motivational cover on it and smiled.

It had taken him a few months, but now, he was feeling a lot more confident about progressing at his company. Things were good with his boss, and he was on some really juicy projects. His colleagues generally liked him, including that HR manager everyone disliked. He had even had some meetings with the really big boss and had managed to book a few more catch-ups next month. And all this while reducing his workload and even the hours he spent in the office. Work was just . . . more fun now. *"More fun, and less work, is what work is about"* is how he phrased it in his mind. Heck, he had not felt this positive about the future since he completed rush week at his college fraternity, knowing that the next four years would be one big party so long as he did not flunk out! Just a few months ago, he was afraid that he would have to work really hard after his promotion to manager and that senior people would start to notice his mediocrity. But now, he was sure that there were kindred spirits throughout his company who, like him, were more worried about their next bonuses than about company profitability. He knew by this point what it would really take to succeed at his company. "This is definitely my kind of place", he thought. Then, he glanced down at the book in his hands and reread the title—*Corporate Success for the Mediocre—A Guide.* "So much truth in so few pages. Thanks little buddy!" he thought, and smiled even more broadly. "The future is bright!"

John Johnson put the book back in the filing cabinet, burying it deep, deep in the back. God forbid anyone should ever find out the secrets of his, and only his, success. He knew that many mediocre people already engaged in what the book spelt out, though, most likely, subconsciously. He saw it around him every day, now that the book had taught him what to look for. But if word ever got out that these methods could actually be methodologically and systematically applied in a corporation, the shame might bring down some of his patron managers, if not the CEO himself (incidentally, also an alum of John Johnson's fraternity!). And, most importantly, it would lay waste his own carefully planned tactics with which he had spent months building his reputation. No longer would people be able to plausibly ignore the manifestations of mediocrity they saw everywhere around them, and he might then not be able to continue manipulating them into thinking he was actually capable and good at his job.

He reconsidered, took the book out of the filing cabinet, and thrust it into his computer bag. Perhaps it would make a good gift for his brother, he thought. He stood up, with a flourish loudly zipped up his bag, then started with bold, precisely spaced, and sure-footed steps towards the elevator bank. At 6:10 p.m., there was nothing more he could do that day, anyway.

Summary Study Guide

The mediocre employee knows that if somebody wants something from him *long enough*, that person will eventually summarise the key points and provide them, saving the employee from putting forth the effort to read and to extract information himself. This book is no exception.

Mediocrity is not a sin. But neither is it a qualification. The mediocre employee needs to actively work at many things for maximum corporate success:

Chapter 1: Results Don't Matter

1. Results don't matter.
2. No one has time to measure real results.
3. Anyone in any position of responsibility will be long gone before the impact of his decisions is detectable.
4. If you are in Sales, results are the *only* things that matter.

Chapter 2: Perception Will Do

5. Other people's casual comments are very important.
6. Instilling a positive perception of yourself in tangentially affiliated managers is critical.
7. Your own manager should be avoided as much as possible.
8. Always accept all offered projects, but only do real work on high-profile ones.
9. Look busy by volunteering a lot. Exploit the action bias.

CORPORATE SUCCESS FOR THE MEDIOCRE

10. Be scarce or difficult to find to exploit asymmetric knowledge.
11. Postpone responding to e-mail and avoid instant messaging entirely as a way to mimic the behaviour of important people.
12. Talk a lot to appear enthusiastic and creative.
13. Create situations where you can look like a hero (with minimal effort).
14. Do everything in your power to seek out high-profile projects.
15. Make your boss look good.

Chapter 3: Myths About the Performance Review

16. *Myth 1:* What is written matters.
17. *Myth 2:* Feedback from your *peers* has an impact.
18. *Myth 3:* Managers wait until they read feedback before deciding their positions/opinions.
19. *Myth 4:* A good review is sufficient to succeed.
20. *Myth 5:* Self-reviews should be objective, including being self-critical.
21. *Myth 6:* Your review becomes part of your permanent record.
22. *Ultimate Myth:* The performance review process is an integral part of the accountability and decision making of your corporation.

Chapter 4: Familiarity Breeds Contempt

23. Do not try to become friends with co-workers. Stay aloof, but interesting.
24. You should readily talk about broadly interesting, but nonpersonal, things.
25. Being self-deprecating is bad.
26. Being funny is good.
27. Seeming actively engaged while saying the minimum is best.

28. At corporate social events, always show up, but leave early.
29. The familiarity inherent in getting drunk together or wearing jeans to work is also to be avoided.

Chapter 5: Hello, Operator!

30. Actively manage the communication flow (what is said as well as what is suppressed).
31. When communicating about your efforts, always claim success and act like it. Treat a loss as a win anyway.
32. Never disparage yourself or your own work.
33. Generate positive messages to convey by pursuing Quick Wins.
34. Utilise the lack of institutional memory to your advantage.
35. Do not wait for your manager to praise you; let everyone, including your manager's manager, know how great you are.
36. Cultivate the promotion committee as broadly as possible.
37. If you can obtain the role of Command HQ Operator, it is very lucrative and easy.

Chapter 6: Wherefore HR?

38. Do not complain to HR.
39. Do not socialise with HR managers.
40. Do not depend on HR to solve problems related to other employees.
41. Use HR tactically against rivals who violate "the rules".
42. Do not try to get HR involved in any processes you manage, including hiring, if you want them done well.
43. Turn up your personal propaganda when HR managers are around.

Chapter 7: Organisational Devolution

44. Exploit the volatility in the organisation and move around a lot from company to company and team to team.
45. Look for opportunities to use Growth Curve Camouflage of successful companies to mask your own lack of performance or to claim credit for growth.
46. Put yourself above the inversion layer where senior managers' performance is always rated well as quickly as possible.

Chapter 8: Female Prerogatives

47. An effective tactic for mediocre females is to claim the inability to do a task.
48. It is even more effective if accompanied by a wide-eyed, blinking stare.
49. Selective defensive delegation can help you get others to do something you do not want to do but requires knowledge of how to manipulate psychological weak points.
50. Wearing sexy clothes does not require any knowledge but can be just as effective.
51. Act caring and motherly if you are in the position to fake it.

In conclusion, I wish you luck, and may your corporate career be a successful and rewarding one. Now go forth and remember: never let your mediocrity slow you down! Odds are most people will not even notice it.

A Final Note on Leadership

It has been fashionable for many years to write about "Leadership" in the Management press. My own perspective on it is very simple and clear but not verbose enough for a whole book. So I include it as a little appendix to this one.

Leadership **is about getting people to do things they would not do otherwise.**

It is absolutely that simple. And, there are exactly two ways to do this:

A) *Convince them that doing it is good, effective, useful, and/or beneficial.* This approach requires competence, knowledge, articulation, and authority on the part of the leader.

Or:

B) *Persuade them to do this despite their desire not to.* This approach requires threatening, bribing, lying, begging, obfuscating, and other forms of manipulation on the part of the leader.

A mediocre senior manager who is attempting to exercise leadership will tend to use approach B, because he is not very good at A. A mediocre employee should, in general, find out what kind of manager she works for and accommodate the way he will manage her: either the rare method A or the more frequently occurring in nature method B. Trying to make your manager fit the way you prefer to be managed is pointless.

And that it is. If you wish to be a good leader, pick your preferred approach and then simply execute it. There are only two ways to get people to do something. And getting people to do stuff is, in the end, the only thing required of a leader.

www.ingramcontent.com/pod-product-compliance
Lightning Source LLC
Chambersburg PA
CBHW060045210326
41520CB00009B/1271